Captured...The Look of the Dog

Captured…The Look of the Dog

Copyright © 2014 by Fern Goodman and Gloria Yarina

All Rights Reserved.

No part of this publication may be reproduced, stored in a retrieval system, or transmitted, in any form or by any means, electronic, mechanical, photocopying, recording, or otherwise, without the written permission of the authors.

First published by Dog Ear Publishing
4010 W. 86th Street, Ste H
Indianapolis, IN 46268
www.dogearpublishing.net

ISBN: 978-1-4575-3207-8

Library of Congress Control Number: has been applied for

This book is printed on acid-free paper.

This is a book of fiction. Mention of specific people, companies, or organizations in this book does not imply endorsement of this book or its authors.

To protect the anonymity of the animals depicted in this book the names may or may not be their real names or who they were named after.

The gratuitous use of well-known names is a shameless method to entice these said well-known people to buy this book. Any resemblance to actual events, locales, persons or dogs, living or dead is entirely unintentional and coincidental.

Printed in the United States of America

Captured...

The Look of the Dog

Fern Goodman and Gloria Yarina

Acknowledgements

From Gloria

I would like to thank:

all of the dog owners, shelters and rescue groups who allowed their dogs to be photographed.

my husband Dave, for providing the computer memory to store my images, back-up portable drives, reminders to use them and help with recovery.

Cody Estes for his continued support. Jane Keller's initial editing, encouragement, and her honest opinion on each and every story.

Linda Hengerer who pointed me in the direction to learn more before jumping ahead.

the Word Weavers of Indian River County for their critiques, and lessons on how to critique my sister's writing.

my next-door neighbor's mother, Lu Krueger for additional editing.

Guy Kawasaki for his book APE with information to guide to self-publish.

most of all, I thank Fern Goodman for a wonderful experience, journey in writing, re-writing and being extremely patient with me. With our numerous phone calls, she listened each time I interrupted her and kept on track.

From Fern

I would like to thank:

everywhere for looking so darn cute

single member of the Seminole County Writers Group, Lake Mary, FL who learned me how to write more better than I never could. LOL

Bubba Lou, for leaving me alone to write.

random person I begged to read and give their opinion, Barbara for one.

of all (yes, me too), I'd like to thank my sister, Gloria Yarina, who had enough confidence in me to invite write about her passionate photographs and transform her words into substance. Our 'go to' phrase "How do people do this alone?" Thank doggie heaven we had each other.

Table of Contents

Our Child	9
The Showgirl	10
Salty Dog	13
Pack Leader	15
Picture Perfect	16
Joy Oh Boy	19
Pure Joy	21
King Size Optimist	22
Chubs	27
Poo Diddy Poo	28
UnKnown	31
Older Dog, She Has My Heart	33
He Only Peed	34
Secret's Out	37
Miss Dancer	39
Charmed I'm Sure	41
Wise Guy	42
Interview with a Runner	45
Pampered Pooch	46
Get a Lil Chi	48
Captain Snifter	51
Park It	52
The Thinker	55
50 Shades of Dachshunds	57
The Right Match	58
Furry Hurry	62
LBD (not your Little Black Dress)	64
Rivals	67
In the Habit	68
Devoted	71
Blizzard's Adventure	72
Ole Blue Eyes	77
That Face	79
Dog Quartet	80
Teenage Whine	83
Bad Hair Day	84
String Bean Diet	88
The Aww Factor	89
Canine Couriers	90
The Aww Factor 2	95
Dog Art	97
Host with Most	99
Beach Discovery	100
Soldier Service	105
Oh, Poodiful	109
Top Ten Phrases	110
Freedom of Speak	112
The Talker	117
Farm Dog	118
Dig It Dog	121
Saved by the Law	124
Beyond Friendly	127
Dog Trivia	128
Rescued Dog Answers	129
Lovitude	132
End of Series	135

Additional Content

Read the Inspiration by Gloria and Fern

Where's Tony? (Fern's Dog) - Answer is with the list of adopted dogs

Play Dog Trivia

Guess which dogs were adopted from a shelter/rescue organization

Answers are in the back of the book

After reading *Captured…The Look of the Dog*, please send your comments to:

TheLookoftheDog@hotmail.com
Visit our websites:
Gloriayarina.com
Ferngoodman.com

10% of Net Profits will be donated to Non-Profit Rescue Organization

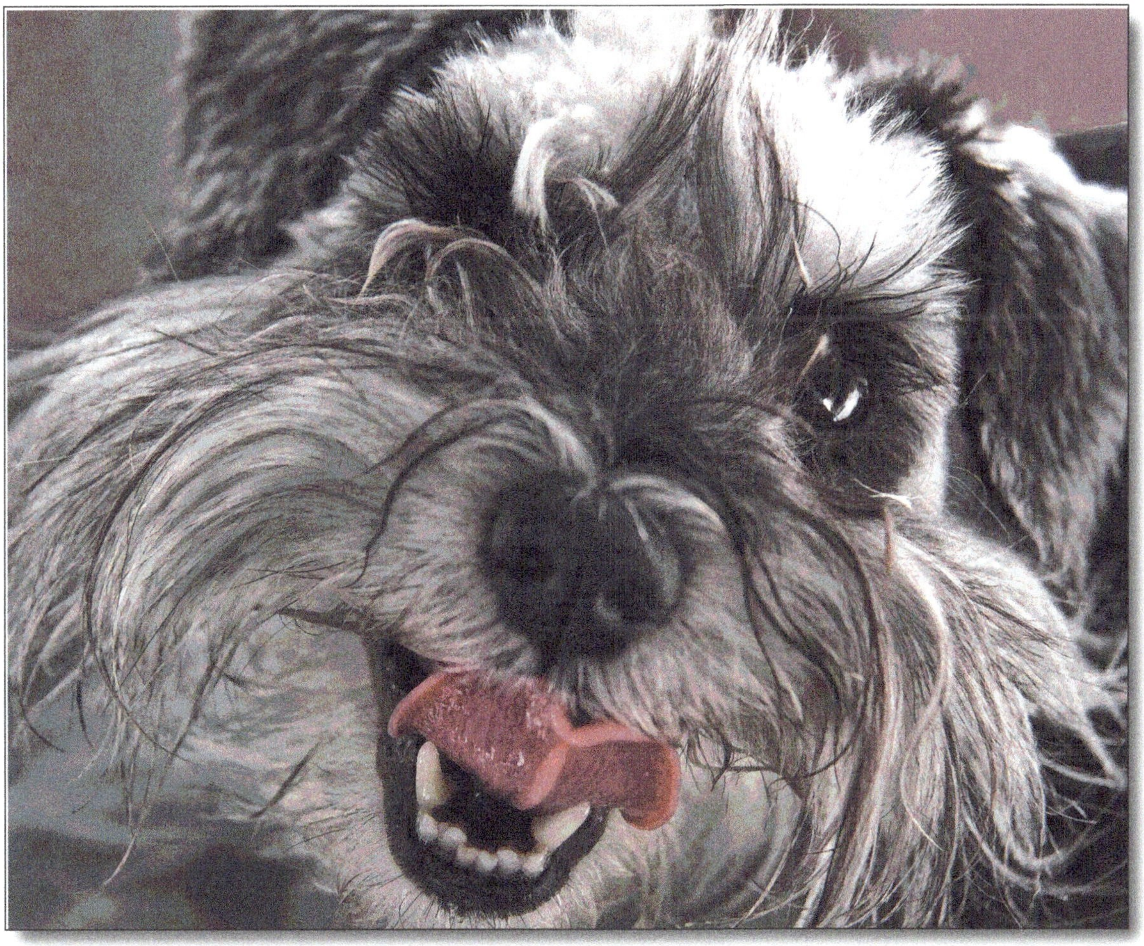

Gloria's Inspiration

Quality time for me is spending time with my three precious dogs. I unwind as I marvel watching them run, hunt and play. They run like miniature stallions; they hunt with a resourceful vigor; and they play with the focus of a scientist. In respite they lounge in the middle of the yard finding a sunny spot by the fence on the cool dirt, under the palms, or by their mom (me). I beam with joy when the three of them surround me to rest on the patio. It's a tranquil, nirvana-like feeling to have three dogs interacting without any aggression or fighting. Sonny, Jen, and Lady are a perfect pack.

Sonny, the oldest, is wise beyond his years. He's an odd looking little boy with a fuzzy cotton ball coat which acts as natural dust collector. Bow legged with toes out, his calm, balanced demeanor welcomes all new dogs into his house or yard. Needing little attention, he's always near, yet rarely touching. Well trained with a Canine Good Citizen certificate he naturally never pulls on a lead. The camera captures Sonny as a semi-happy boy, concerned, sad, occasionally handsome, but always charismatic.

Lady is the opposite of Sonny. As the youngest, she's full of energy and spunk. When she isn't leaping around like she's trapped in a bounce house she demands attention, begging for hugs and kisses. She has the cutesy cocked-head-look of a perpetual puppy on the ready. After requesting to come up by placing a paw on my leg, Lady will give her most heartfelt hug. I know it's wrong to give in but what's a mom to do? She is also my watchdog on guard to give me an intruder alert. Lady is elegant with white fluff on her legs known as pants. She is a fascinating little girl, with brains too!

The doggie in the middle is the beauty known as Jen. She has smooth fur of shiny coffee bean and her eyes draw you in like a decadent bath of dark chocolate. You can't deny her. It's obvious she favors men by her ease at charming them and commanding their attention. Jen's whole back end moves like a top speed outboard motor when she's pleased. Then, in a flash, she's done, taking herself away needing to be left alone. (Knowing her history explains her behavior. She spent 80% of her formative years alone.)

When she sits down by my side, very close, she puts her head under my hand insisting to be pet. Jen looks up at me expecting my undivided attention to acknowledge her adorable presence. As I acknowledged our mutual devotion, I was inspired. I hope you find this book as enchanting as Jen, the muse, and the expressive look of her eyes. *Gloria*

Fern's short version of Inspiration

My sister Gloria called me one day and asked me if I would like to write a book with her about the look of the dogs. I said "sure."
~*Fern*~

Ferns longer version of inspiration

What moves us animal lovers? Does a particular brain cell determine pet preference? Our mother was not particularly fond of dogs; she tolerated them while we were growing up because Dad insisted on having barking protection. Mother preferred human babies. She would fawn over every baby that crossed her path. Couldn't wait for her daughters to have babies…we had puppies instead. Obviously, we didn't give birth to puppies; that would be a very different book. We love dogs—all dogs.

I'm convinced dogs choose their people one way or another. While my husband was at the local Humane Society seeking out a dog he saw online, another dog stopped him by putting his paw right through the crate to prevent him from walking any further. The dog's action worked. In a private screening room this 55-pound dog leaped into his lap. He lifted his pleading eyes to meet my husband's and the look of this dog captured his heart.

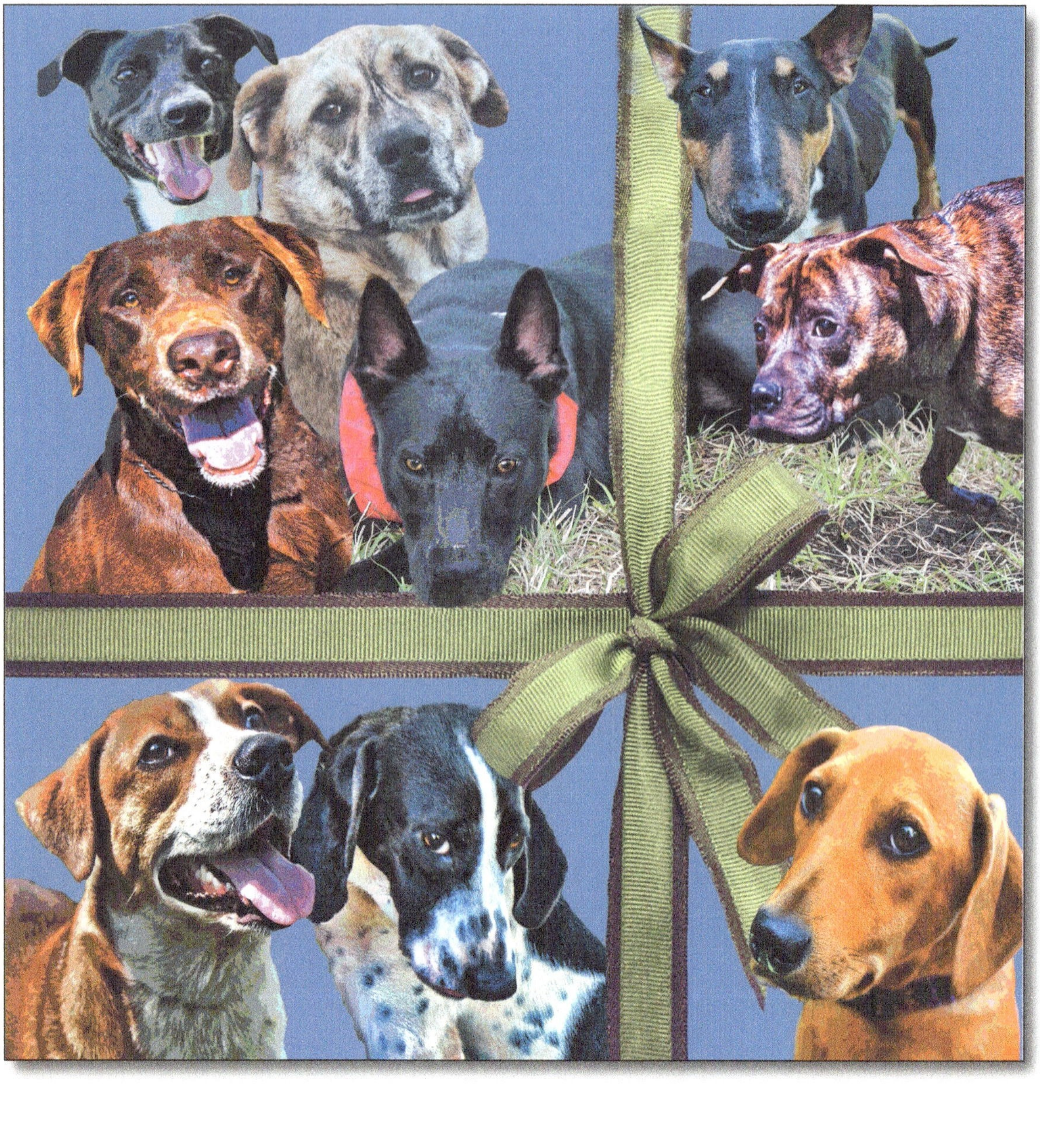

We named him Tony the Tiger because of his orange and black brindle coat. Since Tony only barks and licks on very rare occasions I find myself often wondering what he is thinking. I imagine he spends much of his time eager for a walk or a car ride. He's a wonderful, handsome dog who came to us chipped and trained.

His only real shortcoming is hogging the bed at night. This is the first dog we have ever let sleep on our, um, his bed. We find ourselves in nightly competition for mattress real estate. He is especially drawn to babies and children. Could the spirit of my mother who has passed on be implanted somewhere inside of our dog? It makes you wonder.

Dogs have the influence to give us a healthier, more fulfilled life. Our dog has enriched the relationship between my husband and me. There've been one or two occasions where we stayed together for the sake of the dog! My sister and I have also discovered a renewed respect and connection to each other after realizing our common affection for dogs.

The more love and training you provide the greater the rewards. Take a look at your dog. What do you think your pup is thinking? I enjoyed describing and creating interpretations of the diverse expressions dogs convey to humans. There is nothing like that innocent look or the look of the dogs featured in our book to make you want them.

If I could just get Tony to do the laundry during the day instead of lying around, I would have it made!

Look into the eyes of an animal and you will see, hear and feel a whole other language.

~F. Goodman~

(See if you can find a photo of my Tony somewhere within these pages, answer is in the back of the book.)

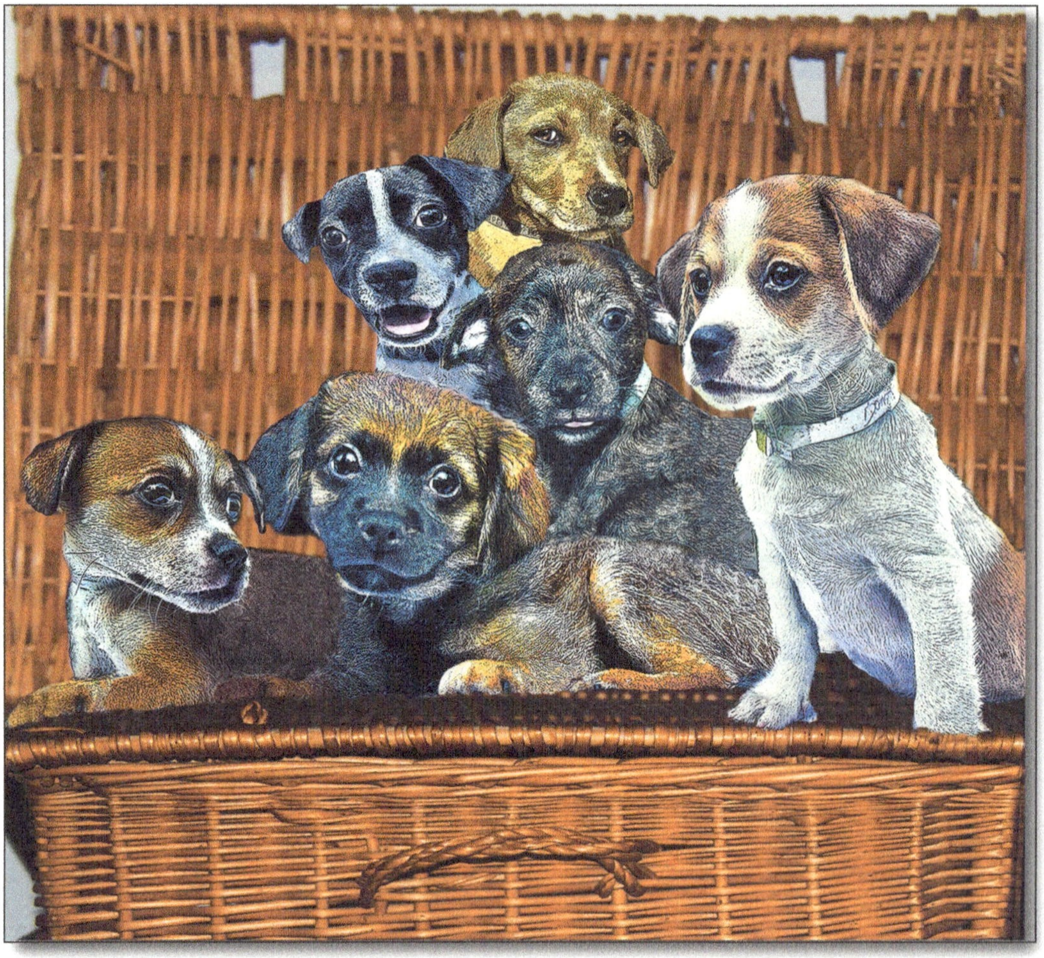

Our Child

I ♥ how you are so human inside the house
One whiff of the outside and it's a different story
You instinctively chase squirrel, lizard or mouse
And prance, swagger and strut in all your glory

I ♥ how you curl your 90-pound frame into a little ball
Next to us you sit, then gone without a sound
We look everywhere belting out a call
Ah, there you are, you stealthy ninja hound

I ♥ how your gentle nature has the ability to distract
The man in the wheelchair whose sister just died
Hyper excited children and fearful women relax
Dogs run from yards away to sniff your behind

I ♥ how you don't lick and rarely bark
Your brindle coat reveals a clue to your breed
You are stubborn, yet obedient, leading in the dark
A proxy son, daughter, the only child we need

But most of all
I ♥ how you raise your head and our eyes meet
Your undemanding look motivates me to truly see
The love, patience, hope, an expectation for a treat
That simple look inspires a kinder, more considerate me
~Dog Mommy~

The Showgirl

My name is Lola. I'm a topless showgirl. I fit the preferred Las Vegas showgirl description. I have long silky tricolor blond hair, muscular body, excellent posture, and am over six feet tall. Actually, I only stand six *inches* tall on all fours, but I have long limbs for my breed. I can do a high leg kick when motivated. 'Wink.'

That's not really the type of showgirl I am. I enter competitions with winning as a goal. *Winning*. My trick is to execute my best impersonation of the Queen of England. I strut, stop, turn and stare. They know what my look reveals; "I am majestic. I am confident." The spectators inhale a breath of awe. Then I smile to show my range of emotion. Everyone exhales and "ah's" with relief.

I haven't always been confident. Training and practice help but even as a Champion I still have performance jitters. I admit I revel in the attention of the process. My owners spend hours combing, brushing and trimming me, to make sure my coat is flawless. I wear the prettiest bows and am always kept safe from harm. I heard my humans talk about insurance coverage on me in case I get injured. I wonder if they would love me if I didn't win shows.

The adrenaline rush of achieving the perfect stack and the conformation jog is my pet preference. But to be crowned the BBS (Best Bitch in Show), that's better that a bowl of chicken treats with a steak bone on top.

* * *

We have arrived at a new show on the circuit. Wow, this building is larger than most, so many fans. I pace anxiously. I fight the urge to do a pirouette because I don't want to mess up my perfectly coiffed tresses.

Here we go into the ring. We do a down and back slow trot. I bet the judge is checking out my very cute, sculptured behind while evaluating my gait. He is thorough, examining my bone structure and shape. My mouth is forced open. His fingers taste like hair gel, don't ask how I know what hair gel tastes like.

They pull the Pekingese and me out of the lineup. We eyeball each other as we reenter the ring and perform additional commands. As I trot off I flaunt my signature look. I even add a right leg kick back. The crowd goes wild.

The three judges confer to make their final decision. The announcement, "The first place winner is Ch Cantina's Ma Lola Blahnic." That's *me!*

I hear the approval of cheers and applause. I glance back at the Pekingese. She's smiling at me but her handler isn't happy. I don't think the Peki's heart is in this business. It's so sad when an animal is forced to perform. I actually feel sorry for the little bugger.

You have to position yourself ahead of the pack and puppy love yourself. That's my tale and I'm stickin' to it.

Salty Dog

I've been out at sea for six months.

How'd you like to bump barnacles?

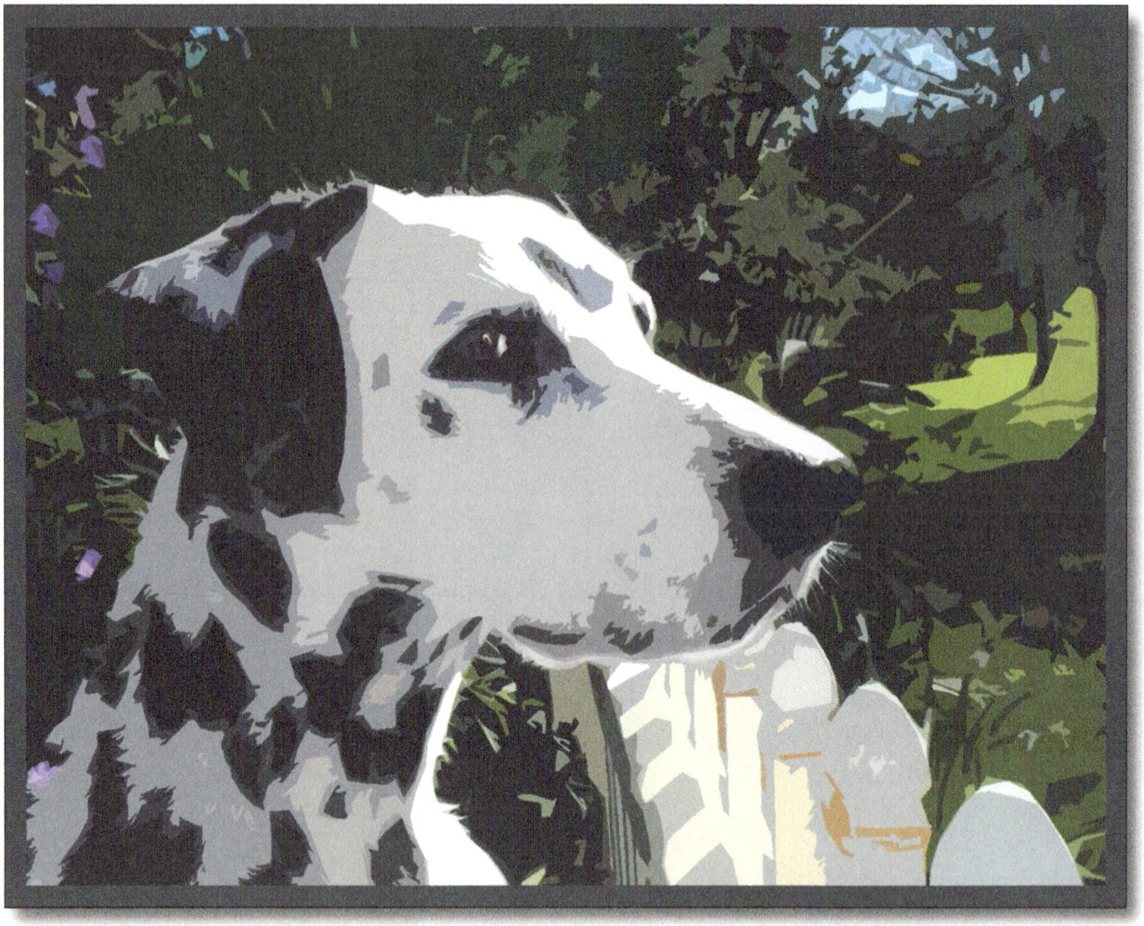

Pack Leader

The other dogs say, "You're not the boss of me."

And she replies, "Oh yes I am you see."

She was given the name Ellen to be

Like Ms. DeGeneres on TV.

"You will not challenge my authority

This is my yard and you will all agree.

There is none with more star quality."

She loves to be adored in reality.

Never leaving the couch when she is comfy

Lets herself out the doggie door to pee.

Invites squirrels to share her favorite tree;

She prances around with her pal Tony.

She nudges you to pet her when your hand is free

Being a pack leader fills her with such glee.

This mutt looks like she comes from a pedigree.

Picture Perfect

*T*oliver is what man's best friend should look like. If you Google "dog" on the Internet, Wikipedia should show a photograph of him (he's not there but he should be). Toliver has a shiny coat of hues found in the most beautiful sunset. His stature is solid, his confidence is apparent as he sits calmly when anyone enters the house. Toliver appears carefree and relaxed. He casually rises to drink from his water bowl, naturally lapping water on the floor. His only thought is to please his masters. He's on the Dean's list of dogs.

As they say, looks can be deceiving. Toliver has a secret, one little personality flaw that monopolizes his life; he has obsessive-compulsive disorder (OCD). The content look in his eyes is induced by the tiny dosage of Doggie Prozac he takes to help control his behavior.

Looking back, he was such an easygoing puppy that the owners were taken by surprise when Toliver was actually diagnosed. The first sign of his disturbance was cute and humorous. The lady of the house was reading in bed when a young Toliver "retrieved" everything that was on the floor and placed all the items next to her one by one. Laughing, she called to her husband and when he entered the room he found his wife in bed surrounded by shoes, dog toys, the newspaper, and all the clothes he himself had left on the floor. They thought their dog was a neat freak and wanted his floor space clear.

As Toliver grew older and stronger his owners became alarmed when larger items were brought to their feet. Anything that Toliver could lift, push, drag or carry with his teeth was an object of agitation. His dog bed would be dragged to wherever his owners were sitting. The dog also never tired of playing catch with their son. Back and forth Toliver would run panting heavily, not stopping until they finally hid the ball from him.

The concerned family tried changing his food, securing him in a crate, having him wear a Thundershirt. They turned to the Internet for answers but nothing worked.

One summer day they were having a picnic outside. Toliver collected all his toys, the kids' bicycles, various balls, lizards, the portable radio and speakers, even the pool equipment. When he could find no more unattached items, he pulled up the flowers and patches of grass and delivered them with fervor.

It was time for professional intervention. Eventually their veterinarian was able to diagnose the problem. Toliver didn't exhibit the normal signs of a compulsive disorder like chasing his tail or staring into space. The doctor asked questions about the family dynamics and routine. The answers revealed that Toliver's anxious habits were a reaction to being left home alone for long periods of time. His behavior in the presence of people was his cry for attention.

He was prescribed a small dose of antidepressant to relax his compulsiveness. It's not known how long Toliver will need to remain on the drug. But that's the secret behind this boy's picture perfect look of a dog.

Joy, Oh Boy

Boy, oh boy, oh boy

I bet you think I'm full of joy

But I can assure you it is a lie

In truth, I'm trying to cough up a fly.

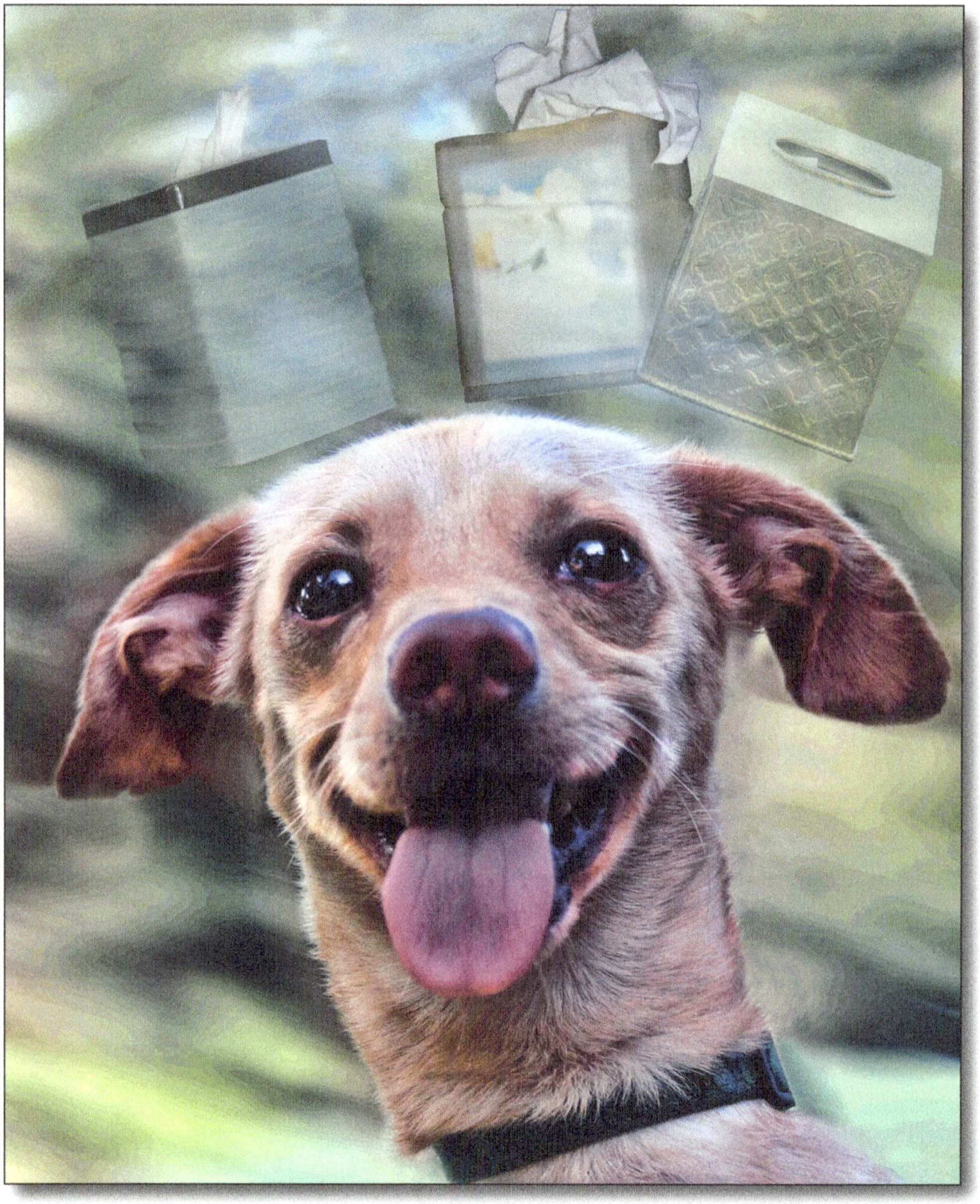

Pure Joy

He is passionate about Kleenex, not merely tissue. That's not really true, any brand of tissue will do. If it's left sitting on a table, drops on the floor, used or not, he will grab it and run, chewing as he goes. This Oliver Twist dog will steal a tissue out of any unattended pocket. A jacket lapel left on a chair, a jean pant pocket, a bathrobe hanging on the door, none of these articles are off limits when a tissue is dangling in view. Unnoticed, he gently grasps each tissue and instantly devours them.

At bedtime he sits quivering as he stares at the tissue box. He tries so very hard not to take one because he knows he would be a bad boy. Alas, there is no doggie 12-Step Program for this addiction. He has one eye on his owners' movements, one eye on the tissue box. Can he get away with it? Desire takes over; he grips the tissue with his front teeth and turns away from his owners. He curls up on the floor to chew his last tissue of the day. His look of pure joy as he swallows his paper victim is priceless. GULP.

King Size Optimist

*J*erry kept his nose to the ground as he scoured for edible scraps. As an active chowhound, he required a steady flow of food, which had lessened as of late. His older buddy, Ben, was small and comfortable like a well-worn t-shirt. They would soon be separated. And Jerry would be leaving his human companions as well. The mortgage on their home was long overdue and the family was being evicted. The best option for the two adults and two children was to move in with relatives. Ben could come but Jerry could not.

The day came when Jerry was led away by a lady friend from church. He loved car rides so he innocently jumped in the back seat. He watched out the back window as the children sobbed into their parents arms. They all assumed this would be a temporary arrangement. As the family faded out of his vision, Jerry shifted his focus. He stuck his head out the window to get slapped with cool air and bugs. His loose lips waggled in the wind.

When he arrived at this lady's home he was introduced to two very serious dogs. They looked him up and down without even a welcome sniff. He was coerced into a bathroom with a bowl of food. Deprived of his usual routine and familiar surroundings; Jerry was too confused to eat. He quickly fell asleep after an apprehensive sigh.

Even though he had his own doggie bed, Jerry was an outcast here. His spunky personality compelled him to make daily attempts to play with the other dogs. He nicknamed them Beany and Meany, The BM Twins, for short. On one particular day, Meany was in a more detestable mood than usual. He snapped at Jerry and bit him on the ear. Jerry yelped with surprise more than pain. He had never been injured before. He was promptly escorted back to the security of the bathroom. To protect everyone's safety Beany and Meany's mom arranged other accommodations.

The next day Jerry was rewarded with another ride with people he didn't know. He tried to push his head out the window, but it was only open enough to sniff the air. The trip became a repetition of ride, out for a potty walk on a short leash, ride, then potty again. His energy made him prance from one side to the other on the seat. A blanket was draped over him as the weather turned colder. He finally settled down to sleep.

He awoke to daylight. By afternoon he was dropped off at a house that resembled his original home. He ran around looking for Ben and his former owners. Not finding them, he ambled inside the bathroom expecting the door to close. Not this time. Nor were there any other dogs. He explored the house again and stopped in front of a window. Wide-eyed with his tail wagging furiously, he turned to the woman in charge. As the sliding glass door opened he sprinted out to a dog's paradise. A large bushy yard awaited him. She followed him outside. He ran around, sniffing the greenery. She laughed at his sincere joy. Remembering his manners he ran back to thank her with a lick on the hand. She hugged him. She grabbed Jerry's paw and introduced herself as Tomesina, but told him that most people called her Tom. She led him back inside with treats. She also had water and toys available for him.

Tomesina lived alone and was actually contemplating adopting a dog when she got a call. It was her sister imploring her to take Jerry. If she didn't like him after she met him, her sister promised to find a foster home. She agreed. Friends of the family were traveling in her direction and were happy to bring the dog to her. Tom believed in timing. Everything seemed to fall into place.

Now here they were sitting together. Jerry at her feet absorbed with a chew toy and she watching his pleasure. Suddenly, as if stung by a bee, Tom jumped up, grabbed her phone and punched in a number. Jerry cocked his head up to listen. He heard the lady's voice brighten and saw a big smile stretch across her face. She disconnected the call, hugged and kissed him. She informed him that he was staying with her, forever. Jerry understood something good had happened. He couldn't resist smiling with shining eyes. He impulsively jumped into her lap. The look of this abandoned, optimistic dog convinced Tom that she wanted to keep him. Jerry had kept hope in his heart and found a home with this new owner. That night both Tom and Jerry slept on the king size bed in the master bedroom.

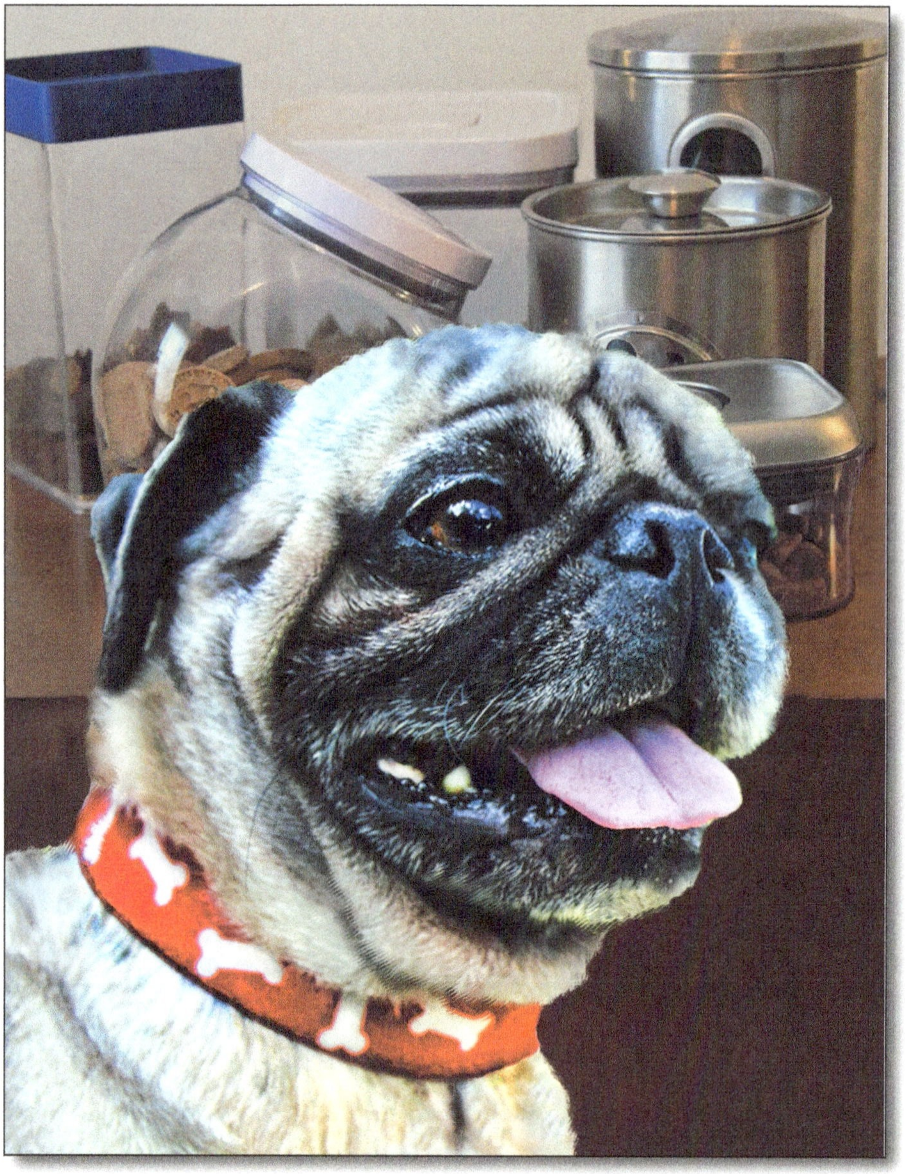

Chubs

Does this collar make me look fat?
Well there's no right answer to that.
I like chow, just about all kinds will do
And I suppose you like cookies too.
I love cookies, preferring the natural ones.
You wouldn't refuse any, you eat tons
You know what's even better then dog food?
Yes, what our owners eat, but that's rude
I don't beg, but I have perfected my hook.
You mean the "poor me, I'm starving" look?
Yup, it works on them without a hitch
Even the lady, she seems like a witch
Mostly the man feeds me snacks at night
You'd better cut back, you don't look right
If you think I'm a chubs you should see him
Oh yeah, he's huge and she's so trim
We get comfy on the couch, watching TV
He slips me treats so she doesn't see.
But what he doesn't know during the day
She feeds me too while he is away.
Neither can resist my adorable charm
A few extra pounds can't do much harm.
But your stomach is nearly dragging the ground
When you lay down you lay around
Human food is not made for dogs
You look like one of those wild hogs!

Poo Diddy Poo

My physical therapist was busting my knots with a shoulder massage when I struck up a conversation. "Do you have a dog?"

"Nope" he replied. "I told my kids they would have to get up and walk the dog four times a day and be home to feed it. I explained to them that they couldn't participate in any after school activities if they wanted a dog. I have my family convinced they don't want a dog."

Being a devoted dog lover, I shared my only negative experience in owning a dog was cleaning their butt hair when they have messy, loose stools. I bragged that my current shorthaired dog always has a poop-free backside.

My therapist said, "You talk about your dog like I used to talk about my babies' poop." If he only knew!

Our pets are our babies. We are constantly concerned about their welfare, their health, does anything hurt, is all well in their world? Dog walks are fine for exercise but they do revolve around their dumpage. There is not a single day when my husband doesn't ask whether our dog, Tiger, has pooped or not. Poo? Did he poo? Huh? DID HE POO? My husband will overreact and want to drag Tiger to the vet if he goes for a day without pooping.

I have the morning shift for poop patrol (his normal doo doo time). It is vital to keep each other informed if the dog hasn't done his business. When walking Tiger we are watchful for his poop pose and favorite locations. Our dog usually 'goes' in out of the way spots, he is considerate that way. He also prefers privacy behind a bush or in deep grass. There are definite tell tale signs when our dog is looking for a spot worthy of his emission. Tiger always sniffs the ground but when he has the urge he is more adamant in his 'sniffering'. Do not dare interrupt the process. He circles, goes to the right then back to the left, crouches, no wait, back to the right, circles, there he goes, coming in for a landing, deep seated crouch and bombs away…

We take note of the consistency of the by-products. If Tiger catches me watching him, he gives me such an indignant look that I am forced to avert my eyes. I shift my angle so he can't see me examining the texture of his discharge. Is there anything crawling in it? Is it too runny? I wonder about a possible cause if the color is not quite right. Was it the pepperoni from the pizza my husband fed him last night? Was it from the new chicken doggie treats? So obsessed are dog owners with their dog's crapola, we accuse each other of giving the dog something too spicy, too rich, too sweet or whatever. Not to mention what dogs find to eat on their own, like other dogs' logs. Fortunately, Tiger does not partake. However, he has a ritual of running at full speed away from his excrement as soon as he finishes.

Some dogs poop, wander off, then wander back and investigate their own poop. They look at it you as if to say, "Hello, human parent, there is caca here and it ain't mine." Clearly in denial, dogs don't want to believe they are capable of generating something that high on the stink-o-meter.

We flush it; they eat it, bury it, expect you to remove it, or they run away from it. The moral of the story is: we use the look of our dogs' defecations as a barometer to their health, same as us humanoids. Poo Diddy Poo? Yes, he did, thanks for asking.

Unknown

"It came to me that every time I lose a dog they take a piece of my heart with them. And every new dog who comes into my life gifts me with a piece of their heart. If I live long enough, all the components of my heart will be dog, and I will become as generous and loving as they are."

~Unknown~

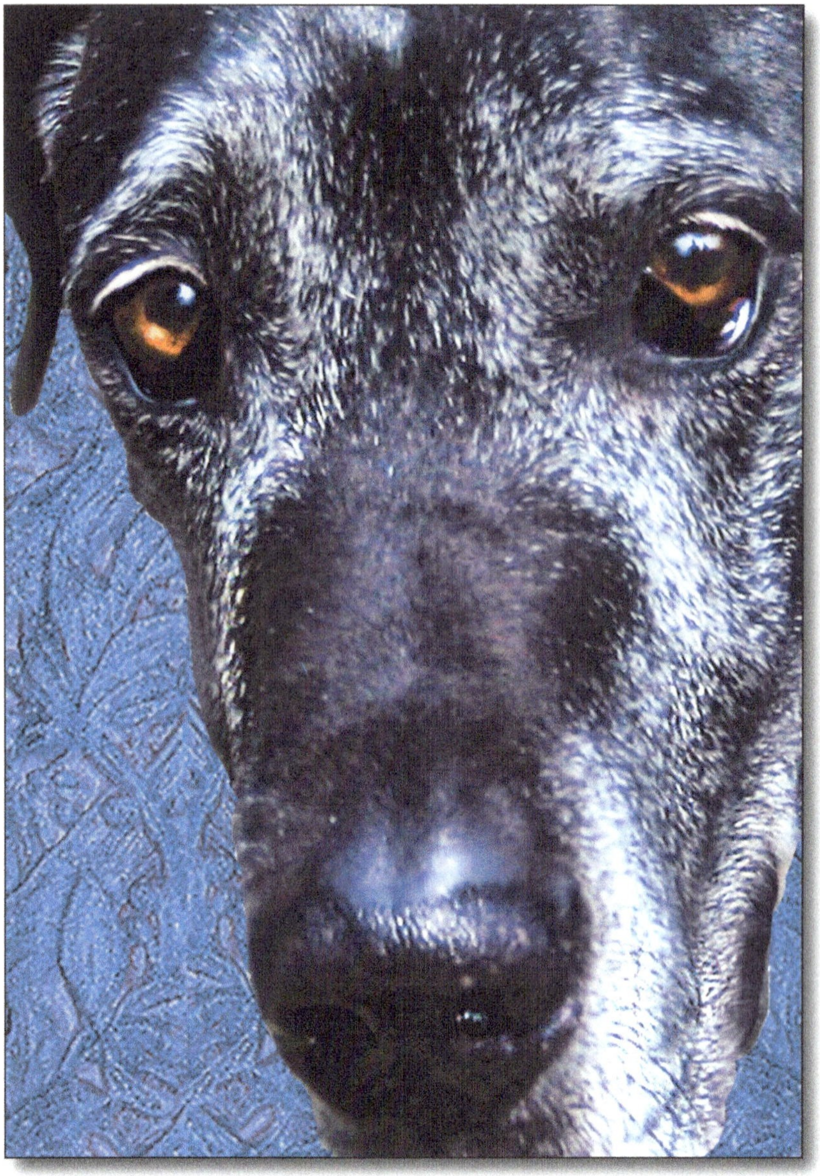

Older Dog, She Has My Heart

She calmly greets me with a smile and tail a waggin.'

She mimics my moves. If I bend down, she does too.

She eats and savors her food instead of in a greedy gobble.

She unconditionally trusts all of her needs will be met.

She snuggles just right, molds her body to mine.

She understands without being given a single command.

She never attempts to run out of an open door.

She knows where and how to communicate her potty time.

She contentedly meanders in the backyard as I read.

She follows me inside when I get up.

She beds down when I am napping.

She still learns new things, anxious to please.

She coos lovable purring sounds when I pet her.

She takes treats delicately, conscious of my fingers.

She walks on a leash in stride; we are two ladies on the block.

She is my constant harmonious companion.

She looks up to assure me, yes, we have that special bond.

She would do anything for me and I for her…she has my heart.

He Only Peed

Why does it happen that 86.4% of the time, I have to pee when I walk my dog? I admit when no one is around I have dropped trou and let it flow. My dog Judd gives me a look of distain, as if only animals are entitled to pee with abandon. I tell him that in some countries men still urinate into holes in the streets (China for one). Then I get the pity look.

We know that both male and female dogs mark their territory with pee, with males being the more zealous of the two sexes. They also leave messages for each other, for example a female dog that is in heat will leave a definite sign she is looking for romance like online dating in the bush. Imagine the entire ground as a humongous chat room for dogs.

Here is a glossary of peediosyncrasies:

High Leg Lift (HILL): most common for dominant male dogs that tend to pee over pee to get their point across. This would also be a signal to any dogs in the area that he is superior. (That's my boy!) Note: It may take practice for some dogs to retain their balance as they hop around.

Lazy Leg Lift (LALL): not in the mood to get involved, just leaving a casual, how ya doin' message. They keep their options open by saving urine for a more interesting pee post.

Lick Then Pee (LTP): to me this is gross, but if the scent has dissipated, they have to taste to confirm that a true dialogue has occurred on that particular locale. This is similar to verifying a missed call by an unknown phone number.

Sniff Aloof Stretch & Pee (SASP): this one is purely for elimination purposes, peeing is an afterthought to exploration.

Disinterested Squat (DISS): same as above, usually simultaneously looking around, primarily females.

Premature Excited (PREMEE): anytime they're nervous or anxious, they can't help it; occurs mostly with small dogs, hopefully they will grow out of it.

Pee in the House (PITH): keep up with the potty training. (Can you spell pee pads?)

Handstand (Handstand): most amusing to watch as they balance on their two front legs while their hind legs are straight up in the air (check out videos online) These acrobats are agile, strong, egotistical, usually smaller breed, can spell out words because they walk while they pee.

Piss 'n Boots: My personal favorite, rare, but it happens. I was talking to my landscaper while outside with my dog and Judd smelled a memo he wanted to respond to and before you can throw a stick you have Piss on Boots. Yes, he peed on the landscaper's grassy boot!

Pee on Owner (POW) and Pee on Self (POS): just know "it could happen."

Keep in mind a combination, variation, or multiplication of the above methods could transpire in one outing. There are a plethora of canine pee mails to answer and not enough time.

I have to get Judd back in the house for his after walk nap. Wonder if he prepares in advance what he is going to "say" during his next pee time. As I walk in the door my wife asks me, "Did he poo?" I reply. "No, he only peed."

Secret's Out

She whispered. "I hear they wrote a book about us."

His answer. "How fascinating."

She excitedly replied. "Absolutely, I can't wait to read it!"

His retort. "Darling, don't take this the wrong way, but you can't read."

She hrumphed. "Hrumph."

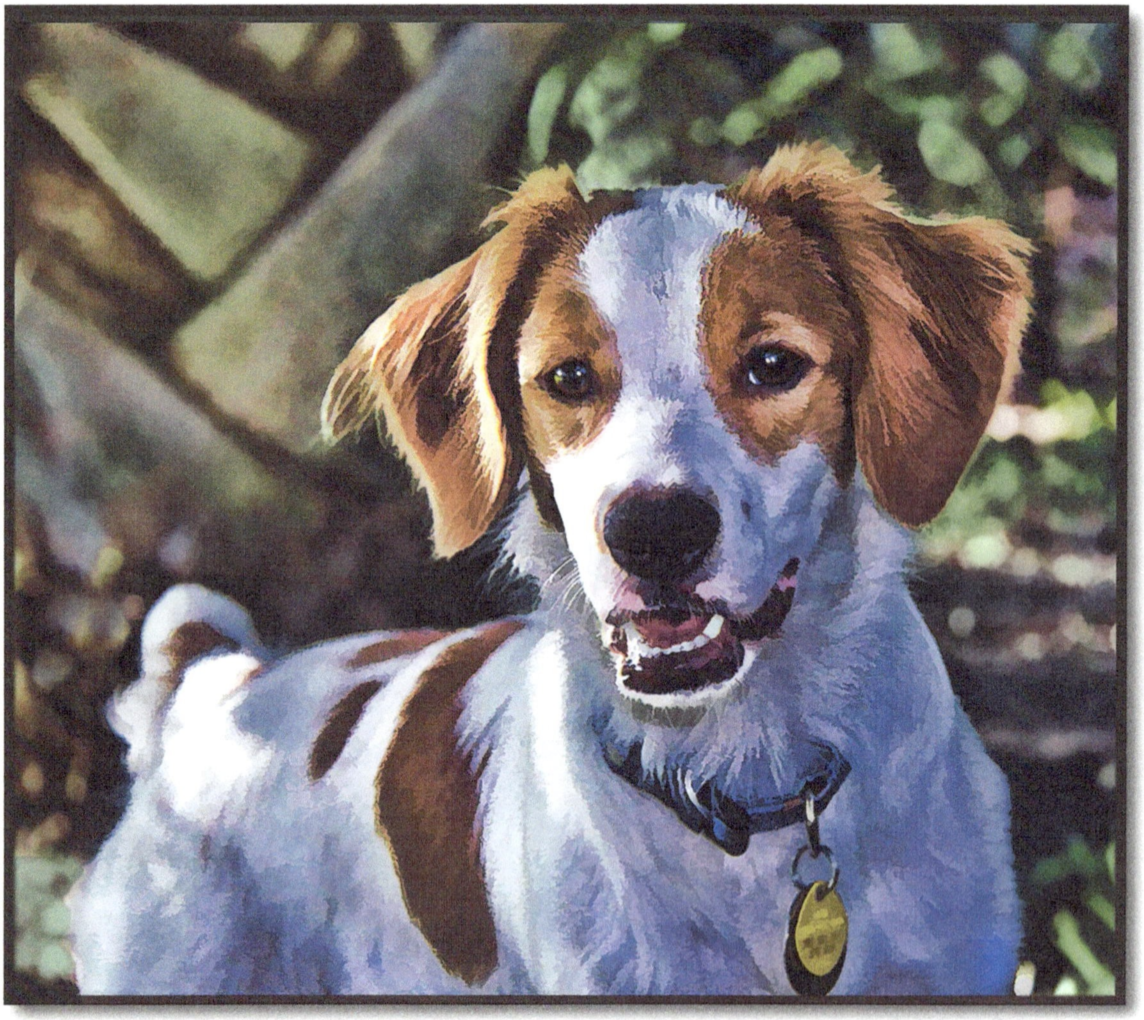

Miss Dancer

She's walking on a leash, head down smelling all the foliage on the way to my front door. When she looks up and notices me, she barks loudly. She's alerting her owners that an intruder is in their path.

They've brought her to me because they know I'm a dog lover. Would I take her in? It's the same old story, them-unable to keep her, me-their last resort.

Something about the dog's aura appeals to me. It's an odd feeling since I've never met this breed of dog before. Physically she's unfamiliar, different coloring, longhaired instead of short, too itty bitty by my standards. Preferring larger dogs, I don't understand why seeing her is like reconnecting with an old friend.

I consider the facts. I have the room; I guess I can keep her for the time being. I can always find her a new home. That's what I have done for other dogs. She's called Ginger after Ginger Rogers because she is such a graceful dog. Incredibly, she bonds immediately with my dogs. She outruns them so they respect her as a worthy adversary. I don't need or want a fourth dog. Yet, it seems this pack is destined to be like the Fantastic Four.

I have to step away and think rationally for a while. After a quick sixty seconds, it's no use; I know Ginger has found her permanent home. She fills a void where I didn't know one existed. She looks up at me and I am in awe. She's the combination of the dog qualities I cherish rolled up into one furry high-steppin' bundle. Well, she does have a dancer's body!

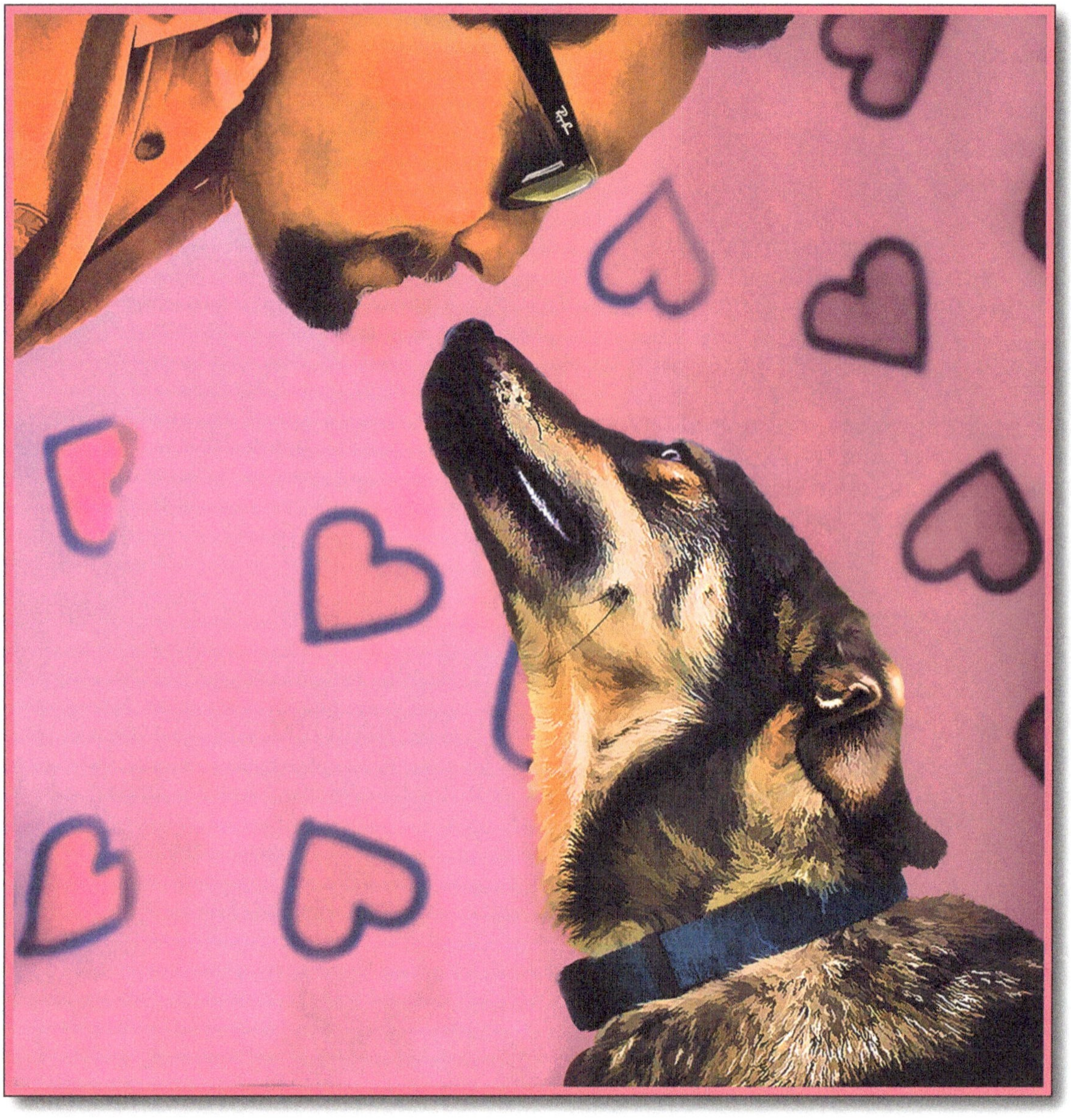

Charmed, I'm Sure

Daddy hasn't been home for a long time. She's daddy's little girl-dog. How could he leave her? She's his Princess. She doesn't like being here with mom and the kid. They're weak; they have no control over her. Their dirty laundry is used as her chew toys. Princess deliberately runs wild in the house, tears up newspapers, knocks over plants and spills her water bowl. When she's not impersonating a destructive tornado, she stares out the front bay window in wait for him to come home for her. They had played ball together, he took her on car rides to the park and rubbed her belly every night. Yes, she had had daddy wrapped around her little paw.

Princess sees him, tail wagging, banging against the wall. No, it's not dad, it's another man. Her momma's been busy. The man is coming in the house. Princess instinctively acts shy, they like that.

This new man puts a leash on her. They go for a walk, just the two of them. He smells nice. Princess does what any red-blooded female canine bitch would do; she gets his attention and bats her big grey eyes. Gazing up at him with obvious genuine devotion, her look captures the heart of this man. He grabs her up and nuzzles her face. She has charmed him in that split second. Now she's his Princess.

I wonder if she gives lessons.

Wise Guy

They were considered the ideal couple, totally in love and in sync with each other (how nice for them). They attended the same college, received degrees in their chosen fields, secured jobs and moved in together. It was time to start their nuclear family: Man, Woman and Dog, no children just yet. Together they visited a shelter, contacted rescue organizations and researched how to choose, train and be responsible dog owners. After their extensive analysis, they adopted a dog they both agreed was right for them and named him Einstein.

For a couple years life was idyllic. Their life revolved around the needs of the dog. They grew jealous of the time each spent with him. Little by little their happy household crumbled into one of tension, unless they were interacting with the pooch. Small disagreements became full blown arguments.

Ultimately they decided it was best to separate. Material things were easy to split up. Deciding whom should have custody of the Einstein - impossible. Both wanted him desperately. As practical people, they hired a mediator. The couple was asked to bring their pet to the arbitration. The mediator listened as each adult passionately pled their case for dog ownership. The wise referee and dog lover continued the mediation by removing Einstein from the room. Each partner was stationed on opposite sides and told not to speak when the dog reentered.

Not knowing what was expected of him, the canine observed his owners in their separate corners. The three of them had been a unit; they all slept together, ate at outdoor restaurants, visited doggy parks, and weekly perused the Farmers Market. The woman stood on her side, willing the dog to come to her. After all, she brushed him, clipped his nails and made sure he was clean and comfortable. With her arms folded, she gave a silent prayer, "come to me boy."

The male was on the opposite side of the room. He was very relaxed, self-assured. He took the dog for long walks and car rides. When the dog was sick or anxious he was the one who stayed by his side.

Einstein looked from one to the other, back and forth. What was a dog supposed to do? He eventually became confused and bored. He began sniffing the carpet. The dog took a stand, so to speak, and lay down right where he was without approaching either owner, face in paws. They all waited. Einstein finally lifted his head, glanced at each adversary as if to say, "What are you looking at me for? Don't make me choose."

The couple gazed at the dog then at each other. The reality of their pettiness left them momentarily speechless, then ashamed. They still loved each other and their dog, what were they thinking? Einstein knew what was best as he gave his most exasperated look to convey his message. The couple simultaneously murmured apologies as they ran to the center of the room and embraced. With his mission accomplished, the dog rolled over on his back with his legs up in the air, head to one side, as he released a satisfied SIGH.

Interview with a Runner

Interviewer: Why do you run?

Dog: Hunh?

Interviewer: Why do you run? What is your motivation to run?

Dog: I never thought about it. I was trained to run. Trained to follow the white flag. I obey.

Interviewer: Do you like running?

Dog: Hunh?

Interviewer: Do you like to run? Do you get a runner's "high"?

Dog: I never thought about it. I do it because it's what I do. I'm good at it and I'm fast.

Interviewer: What's your fastest time?

Dog: Hunh? I'm not sure.

Interviewer: You are definitely focused. Are you genetically engineered?

Dog: Uh, no. I think I'm a Capricorn.

Pampered Pooch

AHHH, I live the good life! My family is very wealthy. Other dogs envy me; people fantasize about being reincarnated like me. I am provided the best of every canine creation imaginable. Mummsie and Dadsie have a chef that prepares fresh meals daily for my delicate digestion. I wear a diamond-studded collar, travel in stretch limos and have my own dog park. For fun I host doggie play dates. My name is Buffet, not Buffy or Buff, and certainly not Buffarino. Uugg. As you can imagine my lineage is pure, just like that delightful Helmsley pooch, rest her soul.

The doggie pillows and blankies are made out of the finest Indian silk. I have my own lounger on the lanai. There's a pool at our mansion designed especially for me; the water just covers my manicured nails. Mummsie and Dadsie once hired a personal obedience trainer but soon realized that it was a waste of time. A dog of my pedigree always knows the appropriate manner to act. A groomer visits me once a week with a pet masseuse in attendance. My toys are all made with organic dye free fabrics of the finest quality.

You must be a member in good standing to enjoy the Silver Spoon Spa where I exercise. They have very stringent policies. Only dogs of similar size and temperament mingle together. I cannot associate with the riff raff. You know those big dogs can behave a bit rough. I could get hurt and I stand to inherit millions.

Enjoy my life? You bet. It may appear that I'm looking down my snout at you. That is so not true. I'm not an elitist. I'm just appreciative of the nice things. After all, who am I to argue?

Now would you be a dear and fill my bowl with the purified lemon water?

Get a Lil Chi

*T*he smallest, yet one of the most popular breed of dog is the Chi…wait - try to spell it before looking… nope you forgot an "h" Chihuahua or phonetically Chiwawa. There are as many types of Chiwawas as there are ways to cook Shrimp! There is a Toy, Teacup, Apple head, Deer head, Long hair, Short hair, Taco, and more. There isn't really a Taco variety; however the Chiwawa that appeared in the Taco Bell commercial was the catalyst for its enormous popularity surge.

During the height of its notoriety, even cat people had thoughts of owning the affectionate, snuggly petite canine. Many were shocked to learn that in reality this tiny dog is also feisty, spunky, and sometimes more than a little snippy. But how cool is it to show off your devoted dog in the palm of your hand? Just don't let yourself be suckered into dressing your Chi Chi like a cute little Mexican Caballero. These pups look to anyone for assistance with their round watery eyes as if to plead, "Help me get out of this ridiculous outfit, por favor. Ay caramba, it is itching the crap out of me!"

These muscular dogs are overflowing with so much personality that you can't help but adore them. Chiwawas are the little big breed, little in body but big in ears, attitude and the biggest most expressive looking eyes. Once they bond, they love big too!

Hey, why not take two, they're so small.

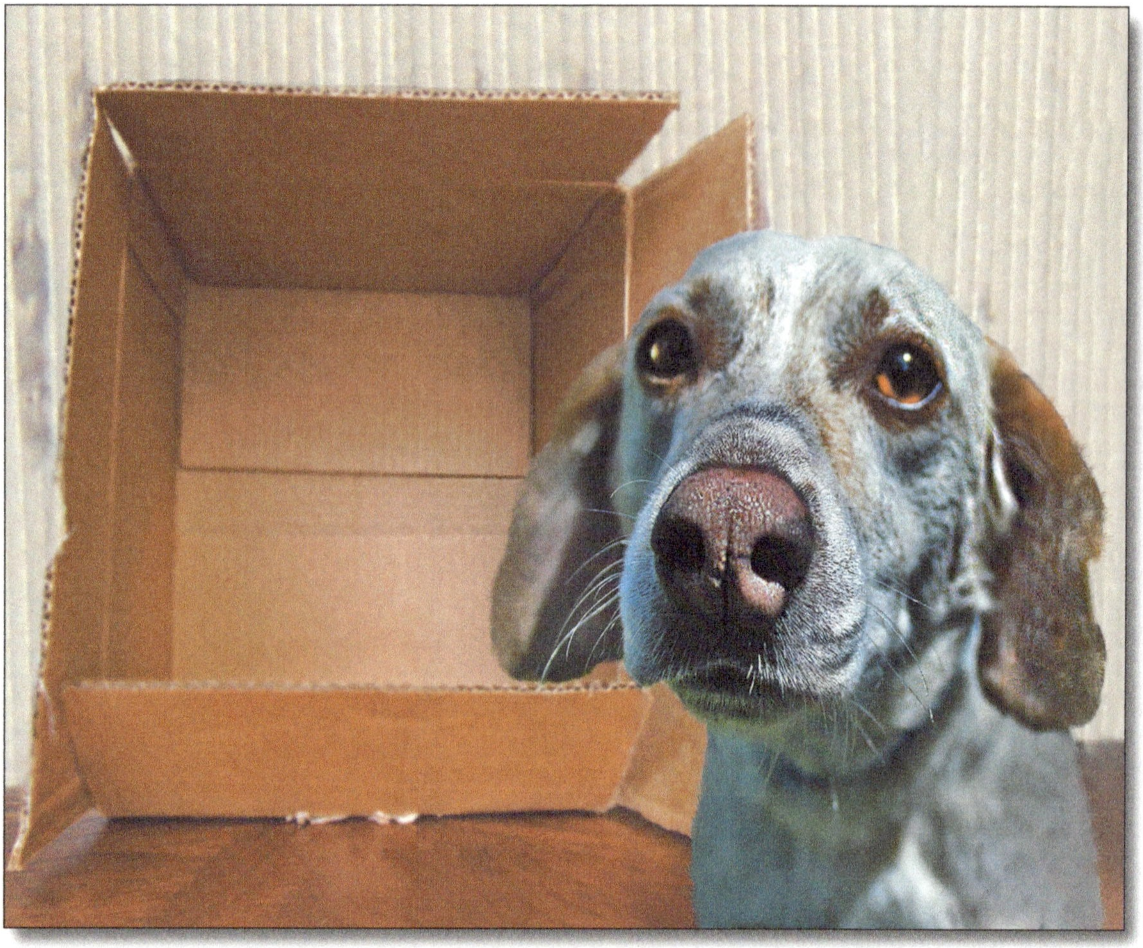

Captain Snifster

Okay, what is that smell? Whadya do? Did you do a stinky pifff out of your behind? Is it your skin that smells funny? No, I can tell it's the same, but something's different. My neck hairs are at attention. I sense danger. I'll scan the room. There's my doggie bed, Mom's loveseat and Dad's lounger. Is it in the fireplace sniff, sniff, no, under the couch, sniff, sniff, no…where in the helix is that strange smell coming from? Did Dad leave an empty beer bottle on the table again? Sniff, sniff, nooo. Is Mom reading a new book or magazine, sniff, sniff, nope?

Hey, maybe they brought a brother home for me? Nah, I would have noticed a puppy right away. Could it be me? Let me bend in half to smell my own butt. Wait. Sniff. Wait. Sniff. Just going around in circles here, hmm, gotta stop myself, snifffff, no, not me either.

What is that over there? It's a large box. No wonder I couldn't find it, cardboard has no real odor. It looks dangerous. It needs to vamoose. Well, the only sensible course of action is to bark at it until it goes away. *Bark! Bark!* I must raise the volume to make it disappear. How did something new get into my house? How could they? I know they know I don't like change. New items disturb my sense of normalcy. I should be present to inspect and approve when anything new comes into the house. What if they don't even know it's here. It could have dropped in from the sky. I'll search for Mom and let her know about the offensive object. There she is, *bark, look, bark, look* We walk slowly together up to the box. To warn her, I bark some more, *get it out of here. It's gonna explode!*

She looks down at me, pats me on the head. Tells me it is okay, I'm a good dog and gives me a treat. I look up at her with pride in my eyes. I did my job. I let her know about the foreign object. I'm Captain Snifster.

Park It

Yippee! Yahoo! Whoo, hoo! We're going to the dog park today. The day Mom wakes up a half hour late every week we go to the park. Same routine. Mom's going through my travel bag to make sure everything we may need is included. She's cleaning my water bottle that has a special gizmo to slurp from. I'm thirsty already. Also in the bag are handy wipes to remove dirt and the slobber from other dogs. We never forget the doggie-doo-doo bags.

Finally I'm secured in my seat belt as we drive to the park. As we arrive at our destination I can hardly contain myself. Banging my tail against the window, I wait to be let out of the hatchback. I bounce out of the SUV. At the gate I sit as calmly as I can and wait for Mom to open it. My favorite pals come to meet me. To prepare for the welcome ritual I stand patiently as the greeter sniffs my backside. Now it's my turn to check out his junk, and we are good to go. As I explore the area, I hope my girl mate (human translation = soul mate) is here. Aw, Ashley and I spot each other. She runs up to me, we nuzzle and kiss, taking off we do laps as a duo going around the fenced yard.

Doggone it, Diesel's here too. He's usually fun, but sometimes a bit rough. Diesel has about 10 pounds more muscle than my 70-pound mass. I can defend myself, especially with Ashley watching. We chomp at each other's face, grunting and growling. It sounds like a battle is raging, but we never touch. A canine martial arts of sorts. Mom calls out to me; "Maxim. Stop! Come!" That's my cue to run away from Diesel. I sit in front of Mom and am rewarded with a small treat.

A young male pup enters the park. I trot off to greet him. We do a reciprocal sniff assessment and a play bow. A pack of us dogs cluster together for a gabfest when we hear a fight break out. Diesel has provoked the newcomer. He is trying to be submissive but Diesel is intimidated by his barrel size and presses forward. The pup yelps as Diesel bites into his ear. A few owners circle the dogs and yell, "SIT!" Diesel pauses his advances, stunned by the sudden human voices. This is just enough time for his dad owner to grab him by his studded leather collar and lead him away. Bye, bye Diesel.

I suddenly remember Mom. I look to the bench where she was sitting and she's gone. I spot her bright colored pants by the injured pup. I run up to the back of her and knock her over happy to have found her. "What the…?" she says. It wasn't her. I run toward the car and turn my head to look everywhere. I start to panic. Surely she wouldn't leave me. I prance back and forth nervously. There she is hidden behind a group of other owners. She's looking for me in the other direction.

I dash off in a sprint as she calls me, grateful for her attention. She fastens my leash and I load into the vehicle ready for an extended nap. Ahhh, there's nothing like a day of fresh dog park air to wear me out.

A rolly, polly homely pup grows up to be Queen of the Dog Park.

The Thinker

"Outside of a dog, a book is man's best friend

Inside of a dog it's too dark to read."

~Groucho Marx~

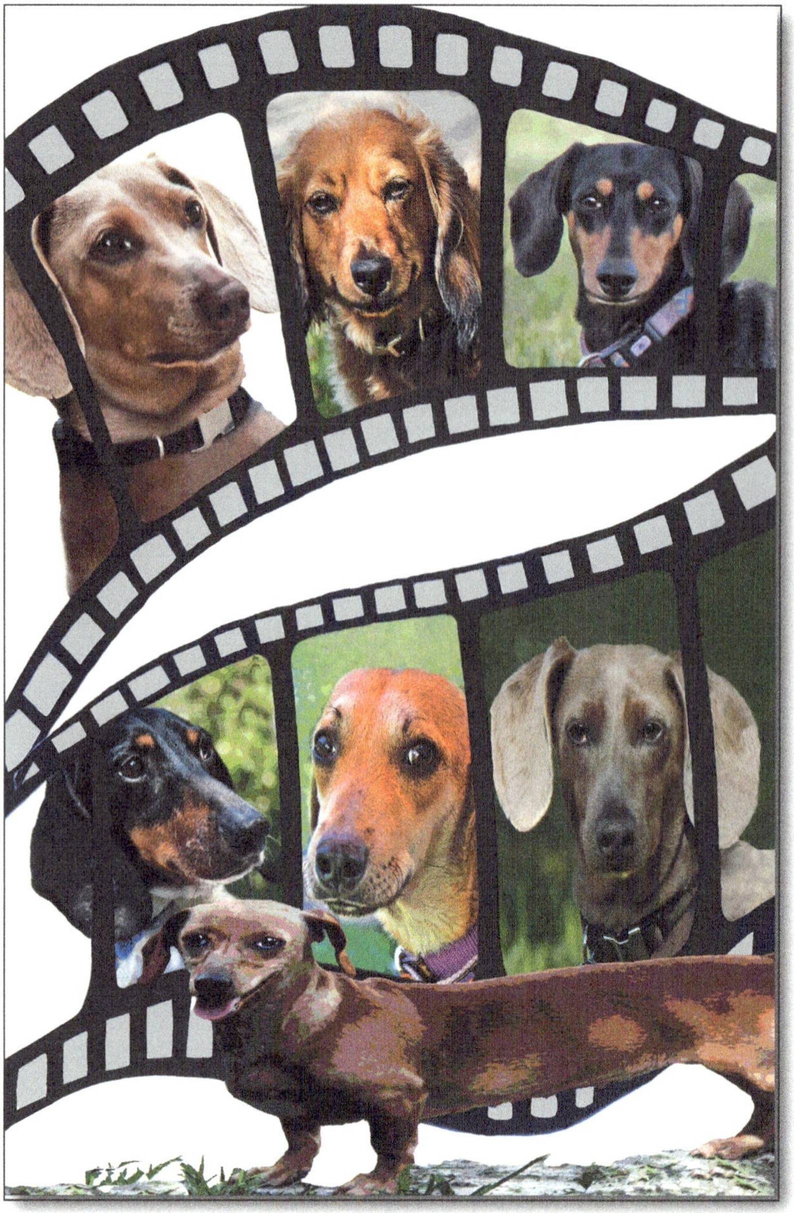

Fifty Shades of Dachshunds

Weiner, sausage, hot dog; the look of a Dachshund always makes me hungry.

One of the most recognizable shaped breeds has been declining in popularity in both America and its homeland of Germany. Originally bred for hunting, it appears Dachshunds come in 50 Shades of Coat, Colors, and Patterns…*Oh My!*

It seems most common tones are smooth milk chocolate, tan or creams

Wirehair in the tint of wheat, Sable and Wild Boar dot their face and feet

In Strawberry blonde or Mahogany Red, a white stripe blazes on their head

The pairing of the father and the "mutter" produces brindle dipped honey butter.

The Right Match

We started fostering dogs after losing three dogs in three years. We could not bring ourselves to commit to adopt another dog. The pain was too great. Our sole surviving dog lived in a custom dog room we built for five. It was a waste not to utilize the space. We heard about fostering dogs so we did some research and chose a few breeds that piqued our interest. We selected an easier breed; less dominant than the dogs we had previously nurtured. We completed applications and were thrilled to be accepted.

On New Year's Eve, the hubby went to pick up the new guy (Emmitt) who was overly hyper for the confines of the shelter's kennel. A home environment would resolve that issue. The shelter volunteers mentioned in passing that Emmitt had a reputation as an escape artist. They told my hubby, "Don't worry, if you stay outside with him, I'm sure he won't leave your yard." Being novice Fosterers, we believed every word they said. Surely our six-foot chain link fence would contain him.

Our lone dog welcomed Emmitt completely. They became playmates. Previous obedience training was evident. He walked nicely on a leash, sniffing around trees; he even knew how to untangle himself. Emmitt was a gentle, sweet boy. We felt fortunate to have this boy as our first foster dog. We wrote a glowing description for the rescue website. Many pictures were taken of this handsome boy with his terrific personality shining through.

Ah, but just like a too confident Survivor contestant, we got blindsided. While sitting outside with the dogs, suddenly Emmitt disappeared over the fence. Once on the other side he ran into our next-door neighbor's garage in search of trouble. We promptly recovered him. We told ourselves his up, up, and away trick was a fluke. We were fooled again. The very next day while doing yard work, right in front of my husband, this Houdini dog climbed again, rung by fence rung. He was busted mid-air, red handed, err pawed, and steered into the house.

This meant I would have to walk him. One rainy day with the ground damp and muddy, he pulled me down, oh yeah, splat! Flat on my face. Not a happy camper was I. We turned to the Internet for advice. One suggestion for fence climbin' dogs was to hot-wire your fence. Off we trudged to the hardware store to obtain supplies to secure the backyard for our foster boy. Maybe Emmitt took his Running Back namesake too serious. We were not entirely confident with our solution, but we had to try to contain him.

The write up describing Emmitt needed to be changed. I had a premonition he was too good to be true. The adoption requirements had to be amended. The home yard must now incorporate a tall secure, solid wooden fence rather than chain link. After many emails from a wide variety of prospects we found a family that seemed like a perfect match for our boy.

We wondered if we would be able to let him go. *Would he want to leave us? Would he understand we were just a pit stop in his life?* The couple walked in. Emmitt met them nice and polite. While we all chatted he stayed close by my side leaning into me. Curiosity got the best of him so Emmitt decided to sniff-check the lady.

He was a people pleaser. She was a dog pleaser who had brought treats. He glanced at me; I nodded and smiled at him. Aloud I whispered, "It's okay Emmitt." Warily, he accepted a few proffered cookies. Interested he looked up at this new lady. She looked at him with total adoration. He never left her side again. As they walked out to their car Emmitt did not feel the need to look back at us. He only had eyes for her. It was a bittersweet feeling of loss and accomplishment to find the right dog/human match.

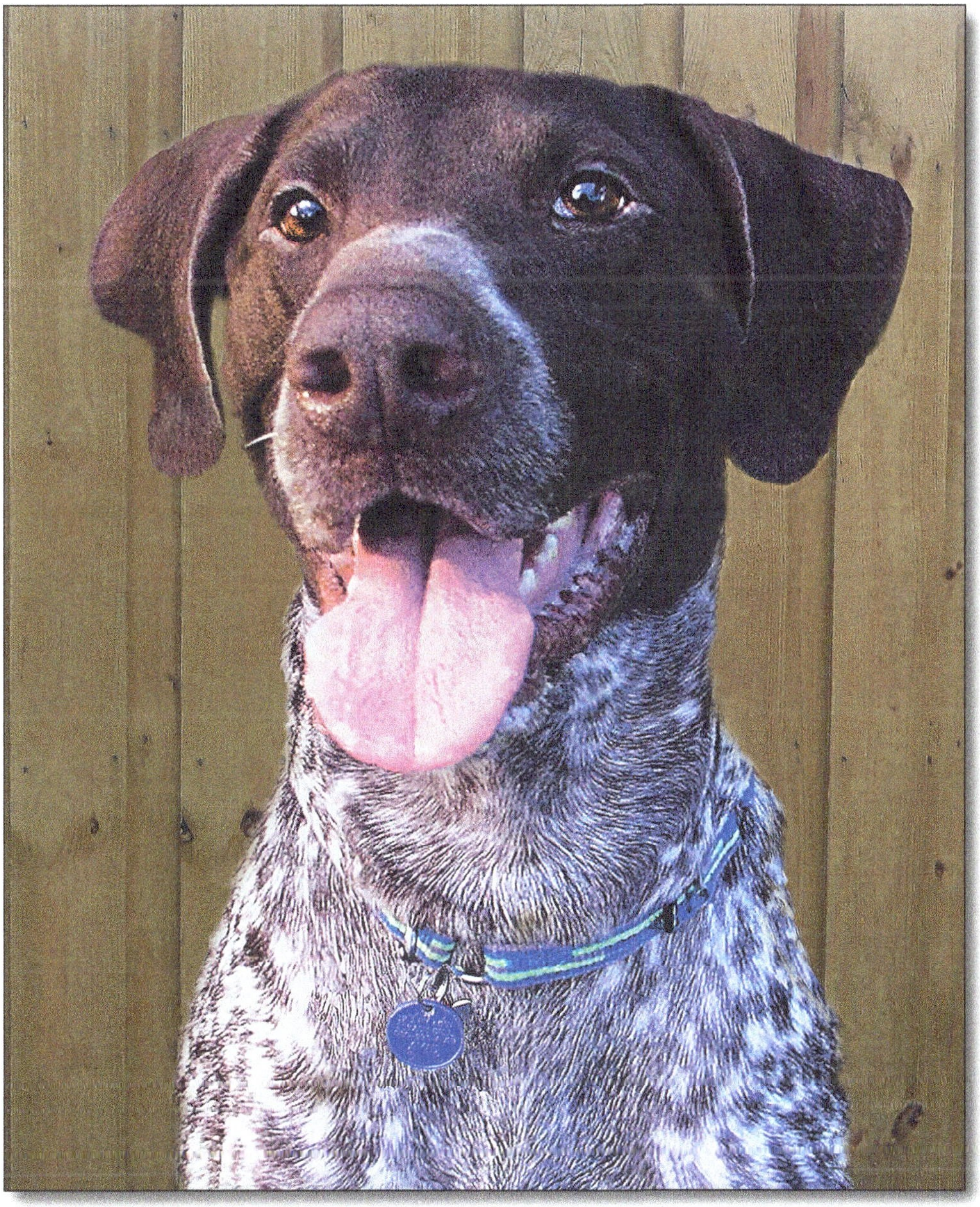

Furry Hurry

It's unseasonably cold inside the house this weekend. A good time to stay snuggled warm under the covers. Uh oh, I hear the clattering of his nails on the tile floor. Here comes the pup, bounding into the room and jumping onto the bed. He's anxious to get outside where it's colder. I can't blame him, for a mammal covered in fur; cool weather must feel quite comfortable. How did he know I was awake? I didn't make a sound. Maybe he heard me pull the covers over my head.

Guess I have to get up and take the boy for a walk. NOW! He is glaring at me. Look at him shaking with eagerness. "*Come on Mom; get moving*" is clearly the message he is projecting as his tail wags in full rotations. He adds a few short whimpers for emphasis. We only get four or five crisp exhilarating dog-romping days a year.

Let me get up so I can go pee. As I enter the bathroom he looks out of the window to confirm that the grass is still crowned with frost. He bursts through the door to see if I am done doing my business so he can get outside to do his. Geez, he's really impatient today. I decide to wear sweat pants over my pajama bottoms and a long sleeved cotton tee on top. I wrap a scarf around my neck, and then add my bulky hooded fleece lined sweatshirt to complete my ensemble. Layers are the key to staying warm, unless you have that full coat of body fur thing going on. I slip on heavy socks, all weather-hiking boots, cell phone; keys in my pocket and off we go.

In the fenced yard, even though I am ready to put on his leash, he runs zig zags at full speed. I wait patiently, and then ask, "Do you want to go for a walk or what?"

"*Yes, pant, pant I'll be still, but hurry up,*" I read his look.

With the leash attached we proceed out the gate toward the sidewalk for our normal morning route. As I walk, I realize that I'm not cold. I'm roasting like baked chicken. I unzip my top coating. I went a tad overboard with the layers. Even though it's February and 8:00 A.M. it's a comfortable 55 degrees in sunny Florida. What had I been thinking? I relied too heavily on my dog's weather forecasting skills. At least HE seems to be suitably dressed.

LBD (not your Little Black Dress)

Opposites play a huge role in our lives. Oddly enough, they provide balance. To laugh and to cry, movement and meditation each create stability similar to right and left, up and down. Well you get the idea.

We named our black Rottweiler, Betty White, but we call her Whitey. Walking her outside in daylight hours versus the night parallels the yin-yang philosophy.

To illustrate:

During the day I stroll with Whitey on the sidewalk outside our community walls. When people head toward us I smile with pride as if I whelped this beautiful girl from my loins. Whitey smiles too and wags her tail in hopes of a stranger's admiration and a pet. Unfortunately, they make a huge arc to avoid any contact with us and we both endure the rejection. My heart breaks as a faint whimper exposes Whitey's disappointment. She adores attention from people and other dogs. Because of her outward appearance (large black dog, AKA-LBD) most are afraid of her. When someone seems the least bit interested I volunteer the fact that she's friendly. Unless they house big dogs of their own they rarely interact with Whitey. On rare occasions I contemplate that maybe it's me they fear. Do I look crazed? I never brush my hair in the morning. I wear any clothes off the floor when the pooch is in a rush to go out. Nah has to be the menacing Whitey, not me.

On the flip side, walking her at nighttime with just streetlights as our friends I'm delighted when passersby dodge any contact with us. My husband tells me that I shouldn't worry about my safety while in the company of a dog that looks as intimidating as Dwayne "The Rock" Johnson. (I wouldn't mind walking the streets with The Rock). The night makes everything look scarier, even Whitey. Our neighborhood is decent, but I'm untrusting by nature. I'm torn between the fear of what skulks in the shadows and Whitey getting the attention she craves.

One night we were on our way back home from a walk to the park and a slow runner came up from behind us. Whitey got between the jogger and me and growled softly, her protective reflexes evident. When he noticed that Whitey had a bead on him, the jogger made a wide detour away from us. That was the moment I resolved my paradox. I now rely on Whitey's instincts. Dogs sense good from evil. One look from Whitey and an invisible force field surrounds us that's not to be penetrated by the unknown. That's hot, right? Or is it cool? Well anyway, IT ROCKS!

Rivals

According to the United States Dog Agility Association, Inc. (USDAA), dog agility competitions are frequently referred to as a 'sport for all dogs.' Dog agility is practiced as a sporting activity that displays a trainer's skill in working with a dog on an obstacle course. Dogs race against the clock to jump hurdles, scale ramps, burst through tunnels, traverse a seesaw and weave through a line of poles in an obstacle course configuration. It's not enough that they finish timely but they are also scored for faults.

In addition to being physically fit, agile and energetic, the look in these dogs eyes is awe-inspiring. The expressive look on their faces is one of determination, and focus mixed with a genuine love to please their trainers. It has become a popular spectator sport because these dogs are so innocent in their quest to win.

One time in a million or trillion the impossible happens and two opponents come eye to eye and have to put on the BRAAAKKES…

In the Habit

I never realized the tremendous value of a routine until I was faced with an unaccustomed occurrence. We lived in a townhouse with a marginal chain link fence around the complex. By marginal, I mean there were openings, cut metal and questionable foliage barriers. My big dog was in the habit of being walked and I was in the habit of walking him. We were habitual creatures. This was a good thing because the property owners were not anxious to repair the fence. I wasn't going to let my pup run loose and get hurt or lost while trying to escape through any of the enclosure's gaping holes.

Every morning I'd traipse down the stairs to the landing, slip into my dog-walking clogs, and strap Jackman into his harness leash, then out the door we would go. Jackman was named after Hugh Jackman who is muy macho, like my dog.

On this particular morning it was a tad chilly. I fastened the five snaps of my jacket and laced a scarf around my neck. I can only assume that I absent-mindedly THOUGHT I secured Jackman into his gear instead of myself. I unlocked and opened the door and we stepped outside. We looked at each other and time was suspended in Matrix-like simulation. Awareness hit us both at the same instant. Jackman was not tethered to me in any way. He was free to run. I will never forget the look on his face. I could visualize the concept spinning in his brain. I think I said, "Oh crap!" But he took action faster than I. To extend Jackman the benefit of the doubt, he maybe heard GO CRAP (ha ha) and took off in a sprint for his life.

I ran after him, prayed and cried all at once because I had no idea how I was going to get close enough to snare him. This dog was a fast one. It was wasted energy for me to run, so I stopped. A couple guys were standing in the parking lot to witness Jackman whiz by them at breakneck speed. They laughed at me as I stood hunched over, hands on my knees, chest heaving, gasping for every breath. Jackman had just turned the corner so I couldn't see him anymore and he couldn't see me. I started to panic then a strange phenomenon happened. I heard the lyrics of the song *Miracles Happen* from the movie *Princess Diaries* coming from I know not where.

The sky became dark except for a shaft of light that shown down on a cement circle that surrounded Jackman. Okay, not really, but it was miraculous. What I did see was this liberated behavioral dog peer back around the corner of the building to make sure his mommy was coming after him. Really? Yes, this cat chasing, squirrel-hunting canine had retraced his steps and waited for me to catch up with him. I approached him slowly not wanting to appear like I was playing. I said, "SIT" in a very commanding yet calm tone. Amazingly, he sat. This time I did not hesitate. I grabbed my scarf, created a makeshift tie around Jackman's neck and guided him back to our hallway where his lead paraphernalia innocently hung. It was then that I broke down and hugged him and told him what a good boy he was. It didn't seem to faze him one bit, but I was grateful that he was a true creature of habit. This was definitely a memorable entry into the gratitude journal.

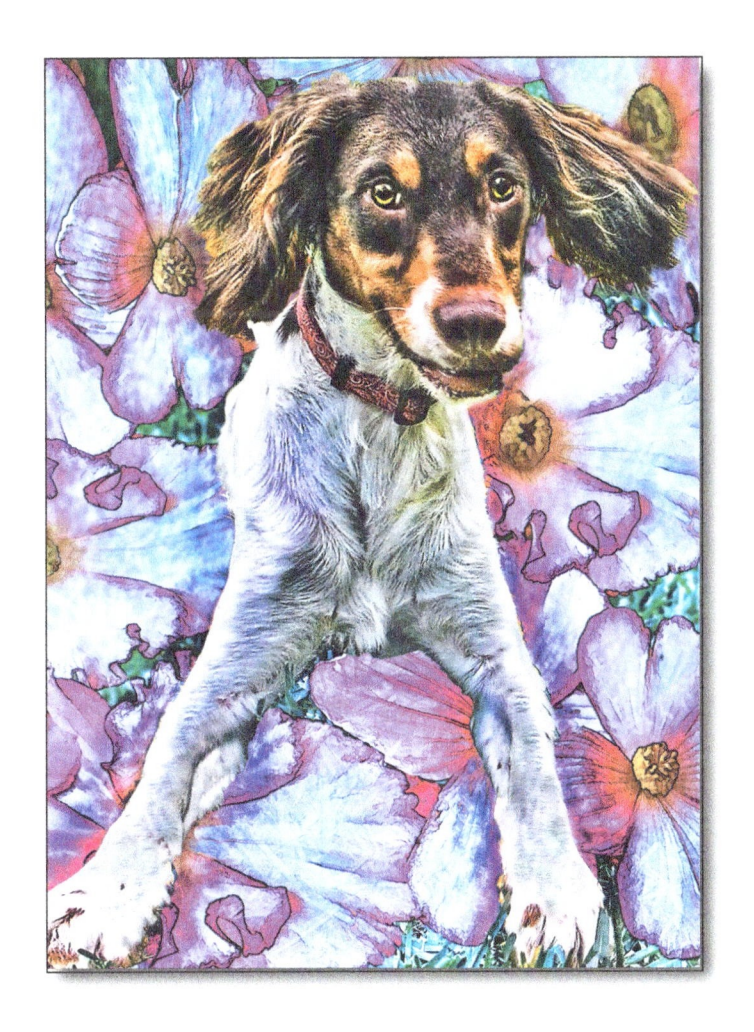

Devoted

"I talk to him when I'm lonesome like; and I'm sure he understands. When he looks at me so attentively, and gently licks my hands; then he rubs his nose on my tailored clothes, but I never say naught thereat. For the good Lord knows I can buy more clothes, but never a friend like that." ~W. Dayton Wedgefarth~

Blizzard's Adventure

*H*e's living in an animal shelter, not really living actually, more like existing. His owners left him to fend for himself when they moved away a few months ago. He ended up here inside these gates with nothing but a nametag that reads Blizzard. The memory of his past life has faded; the routine of this cold, autocratic institution is all he now knows.

Blizzard and dogs his size are being herded outside to play and stretch. After he completes the necessary rituals, he finds himself a spot under a bush to watch the other dogs play. Blizzard is a shy loner pup with little socialization skills. Soon he is bored and falls asleep. He doesn't fit into the "he's soooo cute" or "what a precious puppy" image. Staff members whisper about how pitiful he is, with blond/white hair, an overbite, so timid and unadoptable. None of the employees show Blizzard much affection.

He awakes with a start to find a lizard resting on his nose, but the rest of the yard is empty. He napped so soundly he didn't hear anyone call and apparently the personnel didn't notice he was missing.

He jumps up, excited to explore the yard without interference. This is his chance to pee over all of the other dogs' pee spots! When he gets to the gate leading to the outside, he taps on the metal frame and the door springs open. He looks all around, the yard is still empty, and no one appears to be watching him. The adventure begins; he trots out to the sidewalk with his odd head held high. He observes some squirrels chasing each other in a tree and sits staring up at them. Suddenly he jumps as high as he can in an attempt to catch the squirrels. Blizzard repeats this effort six, seven, eight times. Finally he gives up, exhausted. He rests under a tree until a fly whizzes around his head. This is most irritating. Following the fly, he tries to bite at it over and over, clamping his teeth together within inches of the insect. Done with the tease game, the fly soars away leaving Blizzard disoriented. He is not sure which direction is the way back to food and shelter.

It is dusk, and his tummy is rumbling. He needs to forage for food. He walks on using his sense of smell to guide him along. He recognizes the aroma of food by way of a pizzeria. Following his nose to the rear of the restaurant, the door is open; the smell of baked crust floats through his nostrils. He tries to enter but is shooed away. Sniffing the cement he heads toward the garbage where he spots a pizza box lying on the ground. He is eager but approaches with slow cautious determination. Just as he starts to nudge the box open a cat jumps down from atop the dumpster hissing and snarling. Trying to be brave, he barks in an attempt to reason with the cat, but the feline swats its claws in Blizzard's direction defending its territory. An inexperienced fearful Blizzard retreats to seek out other food locations.

He walks along the alley of dumpsters finding nothing but a dead end. He hears the horn of a train, howls as he heads toward the soulful sound. It is a short-term goal, but at least he has a direction. By the time he arrives, the train tracks are bare; the station is deserted. Blizzard is more depleted and sad than he ever remembers being; as his legs give out he lies down on the tracks, not sure what to do next.

In response to a whistling noise, his ears perk halfway. The whistle is coming from a bone thin man, knapsack on his back with a head of the same blond/white hair as Blizzard. Hanging from the stranger's mouth, Blizzard sees and smells a stick of meat. As the man nears him, he puts out his hand for Blizzard to approve. This man speaks with soft words to Blizzard, inches closer and squats down on one knee.

"Hey dog, what are you doing all the way out here? You shouldn't be lying on the train tracks? How about I share my beef jerky with you? Come on, boy."

Blizzard's ears are now fully upright, grateful he follows the holder of his next meal. They settle on a bench by an overhead building light, sharing dinner. When the food is gone, Blizzard stares at the stranger who looks familiar to him. Impulsively he jumps onto this man's lap, stands bracing his front paws on the man's shoulders; he licks his face. Not having much human attention, Blizzard has never been this near a stranger before. They are eye to eye as they judge each other. The man notices Blizzard's nametag, reads it out loud; Blizzard hears the joyful sound of the man's laugh. "I can't believe this, your name is Blizzard and my friends call me Wizard! We're meant to find each other." Blizzard agrees; they're destined to be survivors together.

Disclaimer: The shelter described in this story is not meant to be representative or customary.

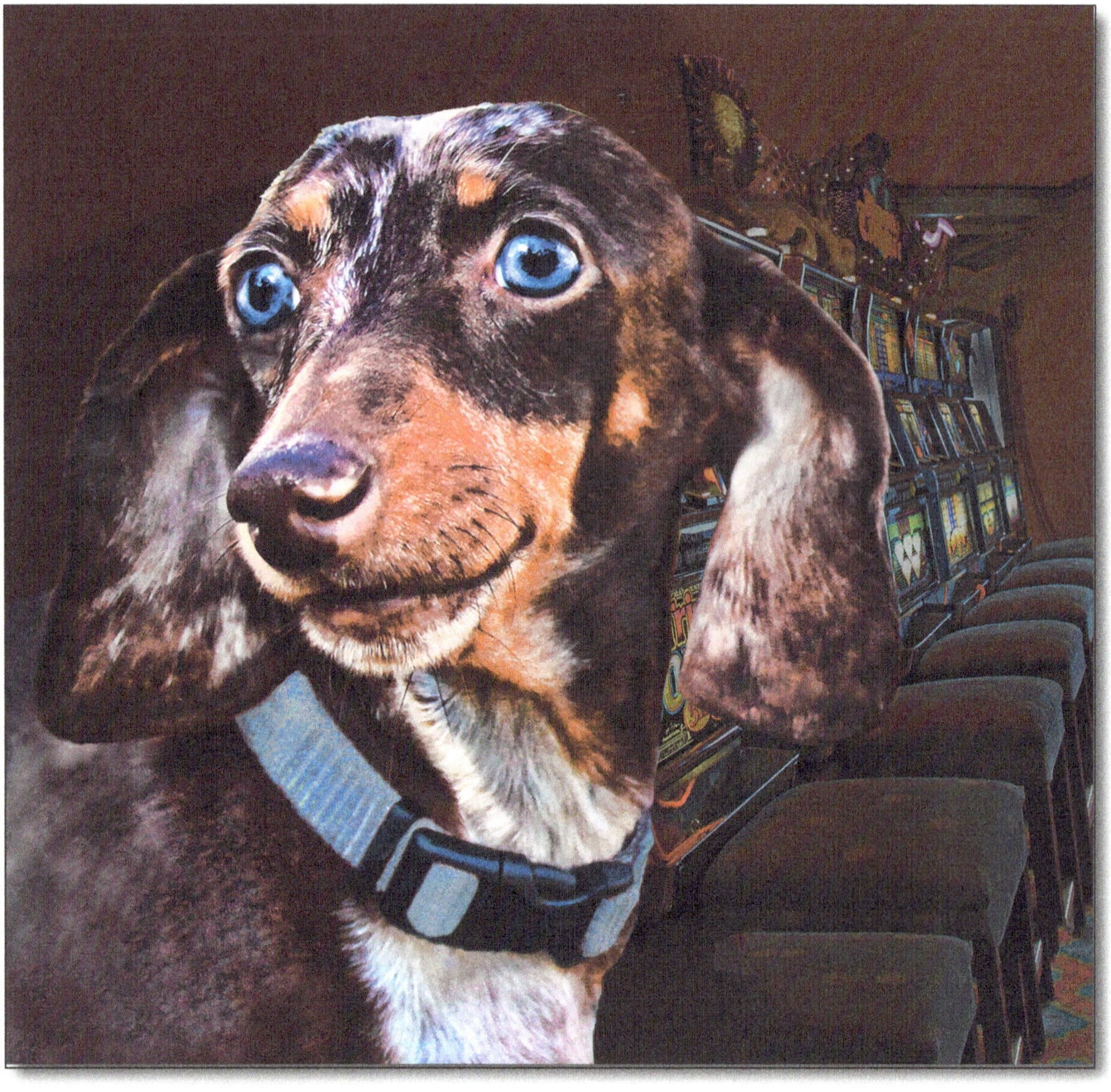

Ole Blue Eyes

The pup has blue eyes
That's quite a surprise
They're even oversize
I imagined brown eyes

The pup has blue eyes
You can hear its cries
I have to buy supplies
To go with blue eyes

The pup has blue eyes
I need you to advise
Can I feed French fries
To my pup with blue eyes

The pup has blue eyes
On only me it relies
As it yawns and it sighs
In my arms with blue eyes
I'll name him Frank.

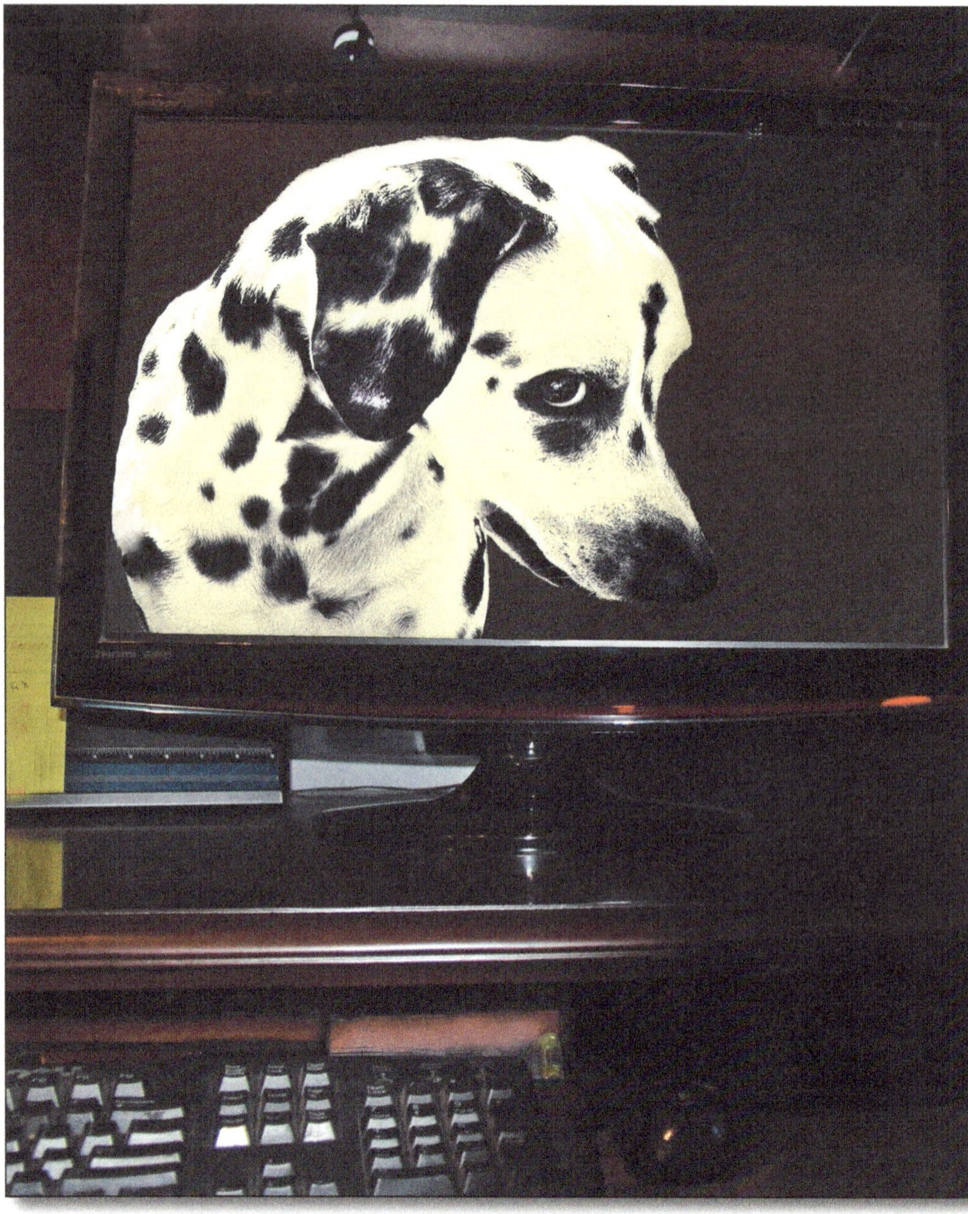

That Face

I kill time on the computer perusing various doggie websites. I do this way too often. From breed to breed I go, to explore all different types of dogs. I'm a dog nerd. This is my idea of entertainment. On this day I see a face. It's a wonderful face, absolutely gorgeous. For some unknown reason I bookmark this page. It's difficult to pull myself away from the monitor. But I do. I go on with my day, work, errands and naturally attending to my dogs.

I go back to the computer to check my mail and find myself viewing that face. I make a salad for dinner and the lettuce forms an image of that dog. I watch my recorded TV shows and that dog's face is on the screen. I realize I'm obsessed with that face. The eyes, the color, the pose; the look of that dog is haunting me. Before I know it I'm scrutinizing the picture, twice a day, three times. How did it get hourly? I cannot rationalize my fascination.

The next morning I wake up late feeling compelled to rush to the computer to look at that face. It's gone! I feel a sad relief. Someone else was also infatuated with the look of that dog's face and adopted it. Whew, glad that's out of my system.

Dog Quartet

Woof. I mean Hi. Rihanna here. I'm one member of a quad of dogs owned by a musical family. We are each named after singers our humans admire. Ironically, all four of us dogs love squeaky, noisy toys. We play with them in different ways. Allow me to expHound.

I love to hear the squeaks. 'Loud and proud' is my motto. The more music I create the better. Simply by clamping my canine teeth (named after us dogs) on the body parts of stuffed animals, I produce my sound.

What joy it is to go running around the house creating noise with absolute abandon. Each squeeze, whether it is on the top, middle or bottom of the toy, has a slightly different tone. It's a concerto to my ears.

My fur-brother, Bruno, has a fondness for the chenille type toys. He is very gentle with them. We think he's a weenie dog, but our owners think he's sweet. He delicately carries his toys around the house then hides them. Hiding them from us is pointless; we're the same species with the same sense of smell. Sometimes he guards the toy under his body as he naps. When the mood hits him, Bruno runs outside and buries his treasure when he thinks we're not looking. That's our clueless, but loveable brother.

Fergie's a true sista who's most like me. She's a young hunting dog who likes to find the source of the squeak and rip it out like a heart. The stuffing goes flying like useless internal organs. She gets the Tuff toys but still manages to obliterate the offending plastic balloon of blare. We all give her plenty of room to split and shred, lest she mistakes one of our paws as the item of her pitchy destruction. Luckily Mom's shoes don't squeak.

Then there's the oldest bitch, Madonna. She enjoys retrieving the toys using a throw-and- go method. She's a big tease. She carries her treasure to Mom, Dad, child or one of us and honks it in our face daring us to grab it. She stands just out of reach or jumps back if you move in to steal it. When we're all feeling frisky we gang up on her to torture and tear her inanimate object into tiny pieces. To witness the scene of an innocent stuffed toy yanked in four different directions at once is like watching a tank of piranhas in a feeding frenzy!

When our Auntie comes to visit with her four-legged child, Sheldon, all our racket making toys have to disappear. It's sad. Sheldon is incapacitated with fear if he hears loud noises. The clapping of thunderstorms propels him to dive and hide under the bed. He thinks our toys are monsters. He chews on silent toys. One day while visiting us, we witnessed Sheldon happily chewing on a brightly colored object. Suddenly a string of musical notes rang out causing Sheldon to squeal and run behind the couch. We all gathered around to investigate. It turned out to be Aunties cell phone ringing away. Sheldon wasn't to blame because the phone had accidentally fallen off the table and onto the carpet. Everyone knows anything on the floor is fair game in a dog's world. MINE!

Teenage Whine

OMD!

Seriously you forgot your keys?

4COL, I'll wait here.

Bad Hair Day

*H*ave you ever woken up and known it wasn't going to be a good day? I'm talking about the kind of day where you step in your own poop. That was how my day started. I slinked into the house through my doggie door and caught a glimpse of myself in the mirror…what a mess. Out of nowhere, Mom scooped me up in a towel and plopped me in the back seat of her car. She dropped me off at the CLIP n SAVE, and with only a backward glance sang, "See ya later, Trumpster."

That's me, Trumpster, Trumpsy, Trumpett. All variations of my real moniker Mr. Trump, named after you know who, because of my wild hair. I hope this day is simply a bad hair day and nothing worse.

A solemn looking lady puts me on a table and starts brushing out my burrs, tangles and knots. *OW...ow...ow...that hurts.* I hear her mumble, "Many of these will have to be cut out." I wonder how my fur got so mangled. I bet it had to do with me rolling in that pile of leaves, dead bugs, weeds and clipped foliage. It seemed like a good idea and loads of fun at the time.

I'm being handed off to the nail and bath guy. His job is to trim my nails, his tool of choice being a very sharp grinder. He continues to grind away while he sings aloud to the song wailing from his earphones. *HELLO, stop grinding.* Brruff, too late he went deep. My nails are way too short, it's gonna be difficult to walk. I'll be tiptoeing around until these grow out. He plunks me into a tub, sprays me with water that is way too HOT for my sensitive skin - allergy season you know. As I continue to whimper, (I'm not proud) it has no affect on him because he cannot flippin' hear me! He scrubs my tender body with a coarse, corrosive smelling soap. Then he applies perfume-scented suds, washes, rinses, adds a creamy liquid, and rinses again getting water in my eyes from every angle. I stoically withstand this maltreatment. Finally he towels me off and takes me to another station.

Wait, wait, don't leave me HERE. This nervous, shaky lady has a pair of scissors in her hand. She's the one who is going to cut my hair? *Stop, you're supposed to dry me before you snip.* I try to kick myself from her grasp. I am still wet, cold, scared and trembling so I have no traction or paw nails. I hope she operates like one of those people who shake until they do something really important with their hands, like knitting or performing surgery. I have to pull myself together. I don't want to be a moving target while she cuts, just in case this is her first day….*YELP…Yelp*, that's my ear. She slipped and nicked my ear. I should nip hers. She applies yellow powder to stop the blood. It stings just like that time I got burned with a curling iron, but that's another story. I should seriously consider biting her. She replaces the scissors with a clipper to make a more uniform groom and remove all the badly gnarled fur. Oh no, *hey lady*, the guard came off the clipper…here we go; now I have a bald spot on my rear end, perfect. She's a professional. I'm sure she will make it look even somehow.

She passes me off to another lady, hopefully the last. What more can they do to me? I have never had this kind of production line grooming before. Usually I go to just one lady who knows my name and does it all. Mom must have found a coupon for this place. The lady stands me on the table and adjusts my head through a loop hanging from the ceiling. She pulls out the air gun and aims it at me. *You have to hold my feet, I don't weigh very much*, and here I go sliding off the slab. Just seconds away from strangling myself, she secures my back paws. Whew… that was a close call. She reaches for a toothbrush. Aw, come on, am I being punked? How much abuse can one little runt take? I clamp my mouth shut, no way, José. She gives up and pulls out a scarf instead. After tying it snuggly around my clean neck she deposits me in a crate where I wait for my owner to rescue me.

At this point, I am happy to be alive. I must be looking Poodle proper, after all the fuss. Op, there's Mom; about time I got out of here. I preen proud and tall. I'm brought out to Mom, she turns noticeably white. I see the blood drain from her face. I have bandages on my ear, uneven hair, reddish skin beneath my fur and a few randomly shaved spots on my body. She is not happy and declares that she is not paying for this debauchery. The receptionist calls the manager who takes one look at me and allows us to leave without paying. My mom bundles me up in her arms and says, "Oh Trumpster, I'm so sorry I left you with those people. I'll never bring you back here again."

I close my eyes and smile with relief as I'm lovingly cradled in my mommy's arms. When I open my eyes I am surrounded by the comfort of my warm doggie bed. I jump up and trot to the mirror, thank you, doggie god; I still have my signature look, my *Trumpadour* hairstyle. It hasn't been a bad hair day at all, just been a bad hair dream.

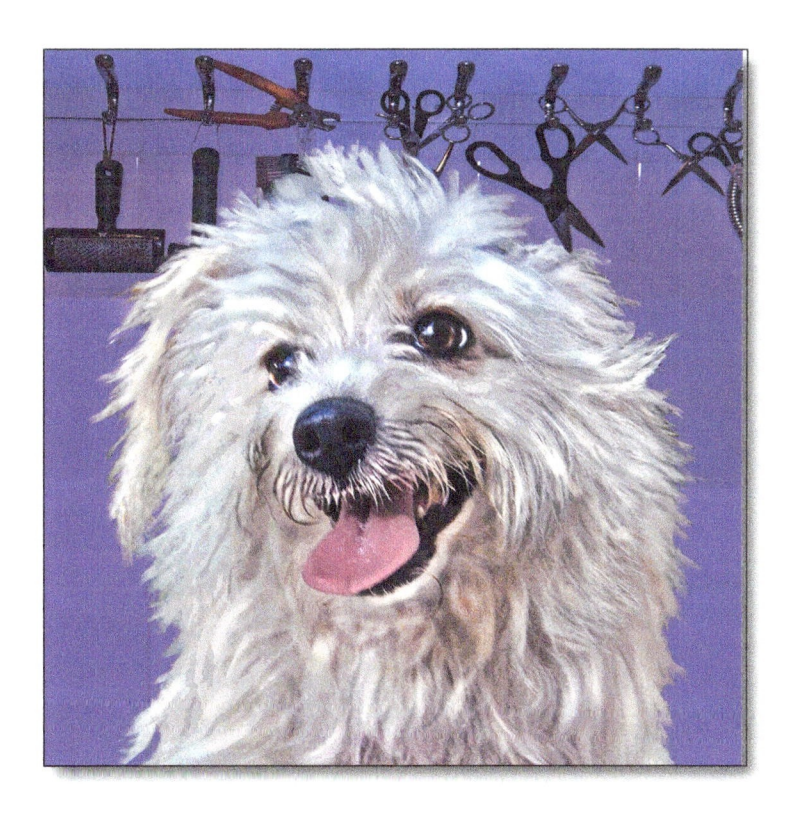

Disclaimer: The grooming establishment described in this story is not meant to be representative or customary.

The String Bean Diet, it works.

"She looks like a completely different dog."

The Aww Factor

Acquiring a puppy will change my status quo

I'll have a devoted partner wherever I go

Treating them right, is certainly the key

I better grab this one before Oprah Winfrey.

Canine Couriers

We ride home in silence, no discussion, and no radio. The only sound is the clash of thunder. We jump at every clap and squint at each vein of lightening. My sister Brianne is visiting for the weekend. We have just left the movie theatre after seeing a horror show. I'm so jittery my hands are white knuckling the steering wheel. I drive too slowly as I scan the road expecting a supernatural apparition to appear. Brianne is motionless with her arms tightly crossed in front of her, probably afraid to move.

I cut into the quiet. "At least the rain has finally stopped, so we won't get wet letting the dogs out."

As I turn onto 20th street I can see my house. It looks odd, misshapen. Rainwater drips from the gutters. A foggy mist hovers over the roof making it appear to sag in the middle. I shake my head to clear the eerie impression and breathe a sigh of relief as the electric garage door opens. No Bogeyman waiting inside.

We step into the house and are surrounded by six joyful dogs. They jump up, barking, happy to see us, eager for attention. Uh, huge problem; I only have four dogs, three Brittney's and a mixed breed. And I ALWAYS lock them in their kennels inside the doggie room. I recount the number of dogs. Six again. My pulse quickens.

"What the…?"

My sister finishes for me. "…hell is this?"

That answers one question. *Am I the only one who sees this*? Frozen in place we look at each other, then the dogs, and back to each other not knowing how to react. As I fight off the shock, I notice the dogs have become uncharacteristically calm. They're all either sitting or lying in front of me.

Oh my God. "I know these extra two. This one is Kurt, the instigator, and the other is my best girl, Goldie. They both died years ago. This is too very weird."

Kurt, my handsome black and white sixty-pound hound pointer mix, had severe hip dysplasia and whimpered in constant pain. We were heartbroken, but knew we had to put him down. Seven months after Kurt died, Goldie, our Golden Retriever, passed on her own from a cancerous tumor.

Brianne says, "Okay. So we know who they are but why and how are they here?"

I shrug. I would like to know that also. As I feel each one to test their authenticity, my touch turns to hugs. I have my old dogs back for whatever reason. My eyes blur as I bury my face in their fur.

Still puzzled, we perform the normal routine and take the dogs outside. A light sprinkle peppers our faces. *Do dogs from a parallel world melt in the rain? Guess not.* The dogs relieve themselves and play for a while as if they all had been together forever.

I say, "Maybe tomorrow will bring some answers for us. I'm gonna go to bed and worry about this in the morning."

My sister retreats to the guest room. I linger with my dogs, one at a time. *Do I bother locking the dogs in their crates? How did they even get out of them on their own? Will Kurt and Goldie be here when I wake up?* For the heck of it, I put Kurt in my only spare crate. Goldie follows me and jumps on my bed like the old days. I awake throughout the night to see Goldie's big brown eyes gazing back at me. *She must not need sleep anymore.* No peep from the other room.

The next morning all the dogs are still in their crates howling for me to let them out. *Why didn't they get out of their kennels again? Possibly because they know I'm home to do it.*

"Anything different this morning?" my sister asks as she comes in behind me.

"Nope," I reply. "We slept and woke up to the same freaky dead dog dilemma. Daylight is when things are supposed to be clearer, right?" *Not yet anyway.*

Kurt and Goldie run around outside barking softly at each other as if they're having a detailed conversation. Brianne and I stand nearby watching. Kurt trots toward the privacy fence. With a brief backward glance he vanishes through the solid wood. Just like that. Gone.

"Holy crap, did you see that?" my sister grabs my arm.

I nod. We both stare openmouthed at the area where Kurt disappeared.

My sister looks at me. "What kind of loony house is this? I have to sit." Brianne walks to a patio chair and plops down, mumbling to herself.

No one would believe this. I don't believe this. Goldie runs toward me, sits, tail ardently wagging. She looks up at me intently, willing me to understand something. I kneel. My hands massage her head. "What is it, girl? What's going on?"

She places her paw on my knee and whines. In a flash I know what this is about. *Of course.* Kurt trained Goldie to be a messenger to guide her daughter Kate to "cross over." I'd read 'dog lore' about Canine Couriers coming back unseen by humans to offer assistance to their offspring.

Kate's my oldest girl and Goldie's daughter. She's a sixteen-year-old who tires easily, wants to be left alone, and whose days are few. I bet Goldie's here to support Kate's journey over the Rainbow Bridge.

Why is it that my sister and I are able to observe this angelic process? Perhaps it's because we're working so diligently as writers to describe the thoughts and looks of dogs. Maybe it's our reward for telling the stories dogs can't reveal for themselves. Brianne made this trip so we could fine-tune the book we're writing together. We each grab our copies, spread our notes on the desk and attempt to work. Our attention and conversation wanders back to the extraordinary return of Goldie and Kurt, overshadowing our creativity. Evening approaches and we give up on our project.

Our focus is solely on the dogs. We prepare a dinner of pizza, diet soda, and banana splits in an attempt to stay awake from a sugar/caffeine high. It doesn't work. I awake with a jolt. Anxiously, I rush to the dog room where I find Goldie lying in the crate with Kate. Both are very still. I crumble to my knees and yell for my sister. The other dogs remain unaffected and my stomach knots into a ball.

Goldie looks up at me as I fumble to open the crate. She walks over and lifts her front paws to my shoulders as if to give comfort. She gently kisses my face, slides down, moves past me and dissolves through the bolted door to the backyard. I glance up at my sister. Tears stream down both our cheeks. Kate has no pulse but looks so serene. We smile through sweet salty tears.

**In Dedication to Mimi,
Fortune's First Damsel,
08-05-1996 to 12-22-2012**

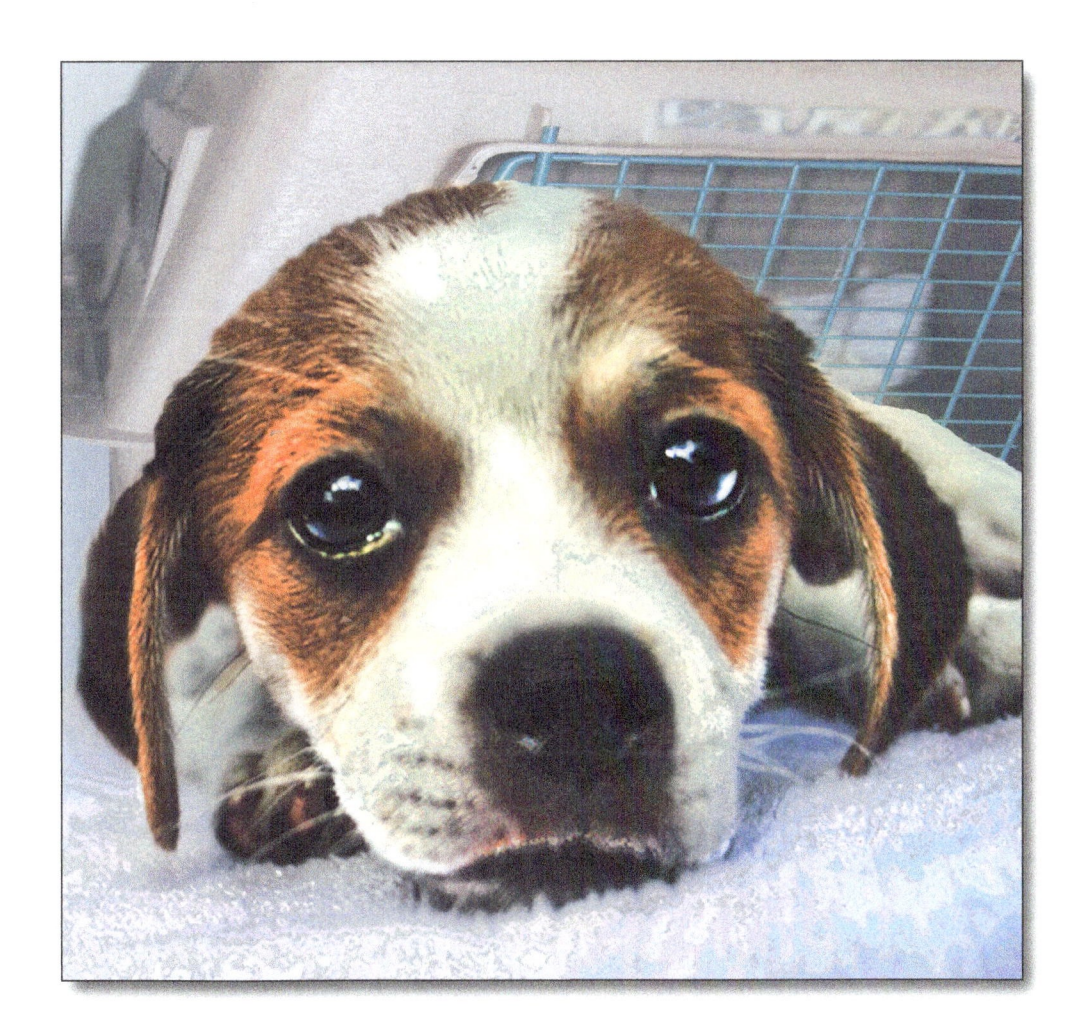

Aww Factor Number 2

A face every mother could love.

The morning this puppy's mug shot was posted,

He was gone in 3…2…1…

Adopted.

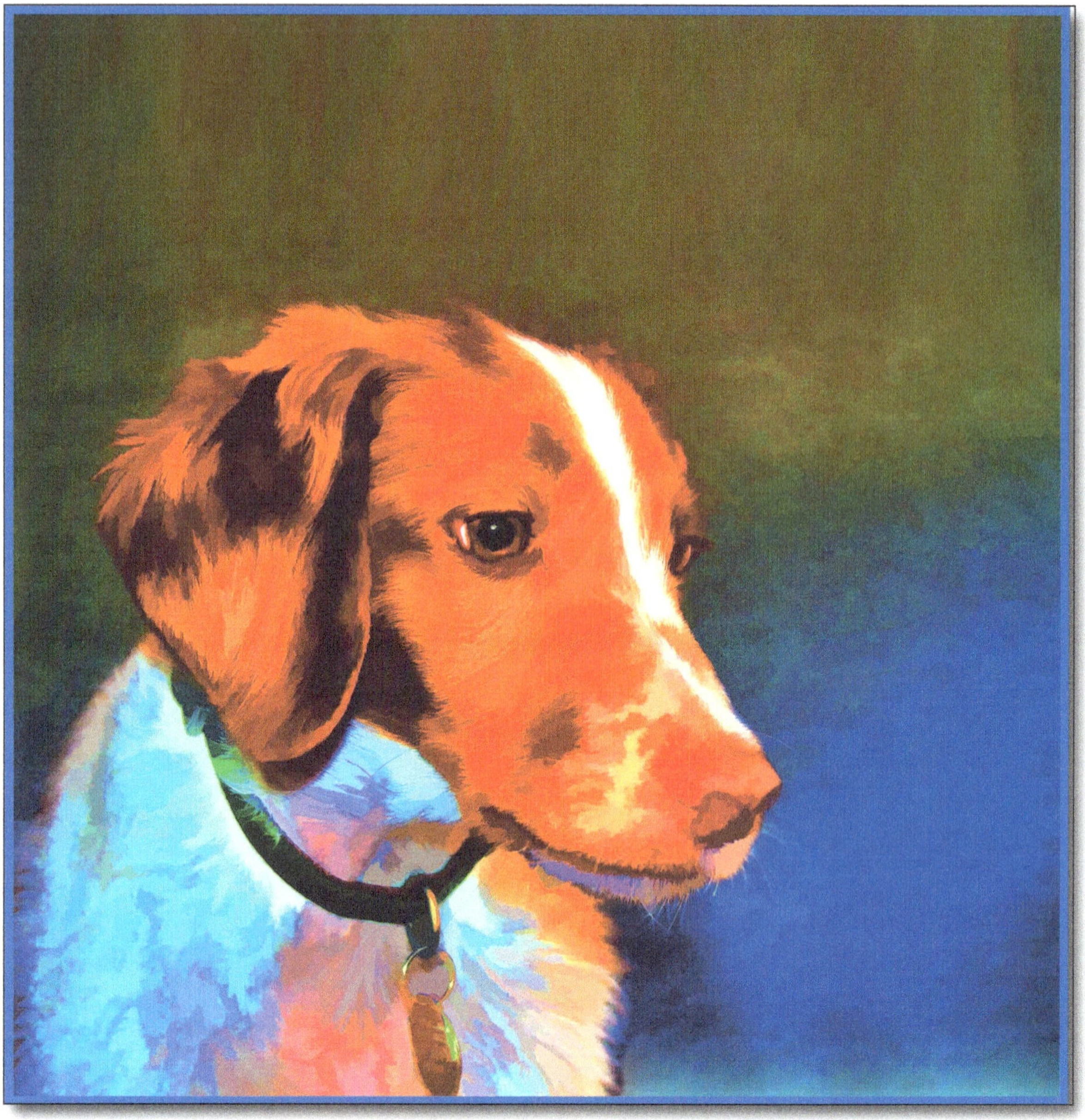

Dog Art

Dogs are steadfast like a treasured work of art

Looking back at you, tugs at your heart

Mold the magnitude of a dog from a ball of puppy clay

Sculpt an obedient canine from the materials of a stray

Paint the façade you desire on a canvas that you spray

Design the joy and demeanor with a detailed bouquet

Dogs are precious like a treasured work of art

The look that connects you, tugs at your heart

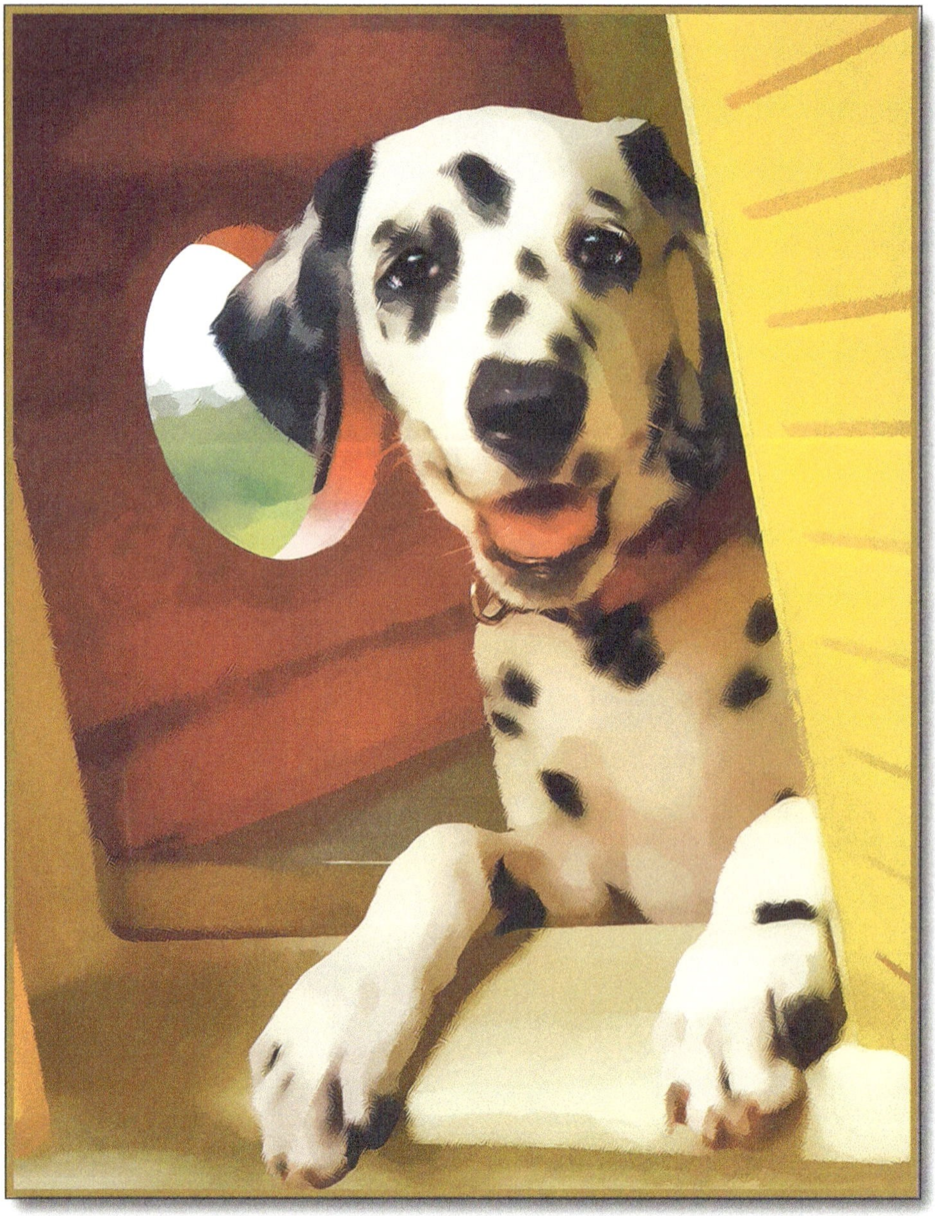

Host with the Most

Welcome in, my friends

to the house that never ends.

I'm so glad you can bend

From the knees! From the knees!

Palmer is my name

you will see I am tame

but you have to play my game

and let me win, let me win!

Step inside and have a seat

If you want, I'll lick your feet

You're required to bring a treat

That I will eat, I will eat!

Watch me perform doggie tricks

Invite all the chicks

I will even fetch your sticks

Just for kicks! Just for kicks!

Wait please don't go

There is more to the show

I guess you'll never know

What's inside! What's inside!

Beach Discovery

"Do you wanna go to the beach, Ozzy? Come on; we're going to the doggie beach." What is this thing called "beach" that my humans want me to get excited about?

How do I know if I wanna go when I've never been? I have simple needs. If there are other dogs to play with, bushes to sniff, and water to drink, I am good to go. I jump in as my owner announces, "All Aboard, Ozzy," as he taps the deck inside the back of the car. My tail wags to imply that I am happy with their decision. Hey, as long as I'm not going to get a shot in my butt, I'll go for a car ride.

With my head stuck out the open window I smell a subtle change in the air. The odors of fish, birds, and the heady scent of wet dog waffle through my nostrils beckoning me like a Dam in heat.

Faster tail wags and whines escape from my throat to expose my anxiousness (I hate when I do that). I'm ready to leap and explore as soon as that door opens. Now they want me to slow down after they got me wound up…I think not, let's just go.

Out of the car on a leash, I lead the way along the best kind of path, lots of greenery on both sides of me. Interesting area. Let's see, a Schnauzer has peed upon this bush, this one has the bouquet of a Cockerpoo, no wait, a Cockertzu, no, don't tell me, it's definitely a Cockerjack. Yep a Cocker Spaniel/Jack Russell mix for sure. Moving on to the scent of, umm, umm, can't be. A male person must have urinated on this bush and then poured beer on it. Bet you didn't know us canines could identify pee by breeds. It's a skill that some are better at than others.

The grass disappears and now we are walking on white dirt. I am used to digging in dirt, but this is sandy stuff like what the kids play in. I'm obsessed with this sand; it magically massages my pads. The path ends and leads us to loads of more sand, now that's what I'm talking about!

Wow, look at all that water. This must be the Ocean that I have heard so much about. I stop in awe. How do they keep it contained? I don't see a bowl anywhere. As we keep walking, I spot several dogs romping and catching a Frisbee in the cool blue. This place is playground heaven. Let's get closer so I can drink out of it. *"NO!"* Hunh? They bring me to the brink of the big O and now they won't let me even take a sip from it. Seriously? They say because it's too salty and I'll get sick. I steal a small slurp to see if they are right… *"NO!!"* Ick, they're right, whatever.

I'm going to plop down here and dig in this lovely sand until I reach fresh water. Wait a minute, holy son of Big Foot; what's that creature climbing out of the water? I look at my owners. They're squinting to focus in on what's coming toward us from the depths of the sea. I stare back at a beast growing more massive with each step. The reflection from its shiny black skin is blinding. As it approaches, it splits into two. Maybe there were always two and I couldn't see the one behind. I don't know. They don't appear to be travelling with any twilight-y wolf pack. Their eyes are enormous and they have hoses attached to the largest water bottle I have ever seen. (Wonder if I can get one of those). Dangling from their hands are large black faceless fish they probably killed and gutted.

They seem to have their sights set on me. I stand and bark feverishly, willing my family to protect me. But no, they actually walk toward these murderous aliens, dragging me with them. I continue to raise a ruckus as the predators remove their eyes and hoods, then drop their lifeless prey. I'm briefly distracted by their abandoned bounty. I realize that it is rubber and not blubber they were carrying. I'm confused. My owners talk to these sea creatures as I timidly look up. A body kneels toward me. I start to recoil, then come face to face with our neighbors Jack and Kelly. Sheewiz, they're so lucky. I was this close to kicking sand in their faces!

I need to come back to the beach a few more times before I decide if I like it or not. How about tomorrow?

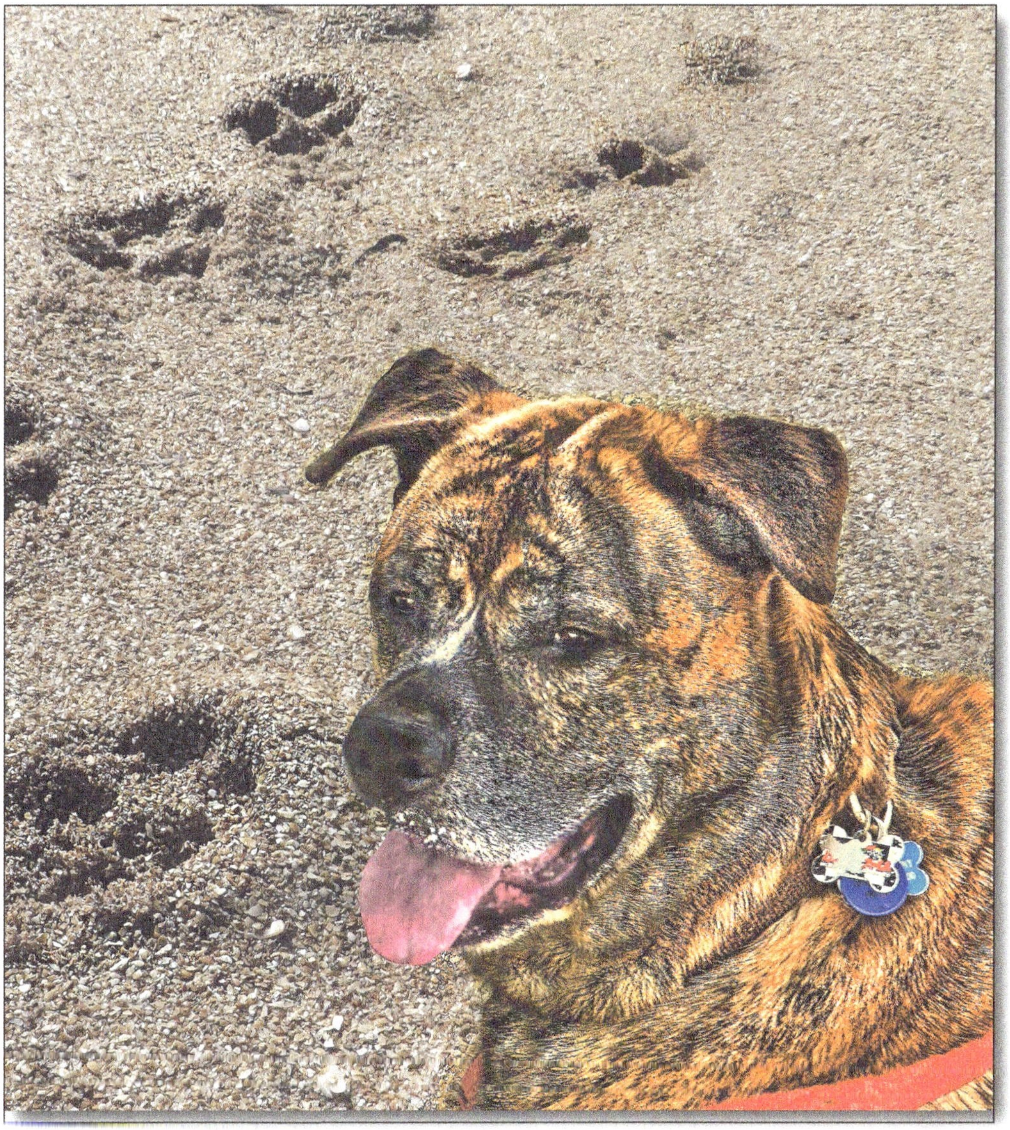

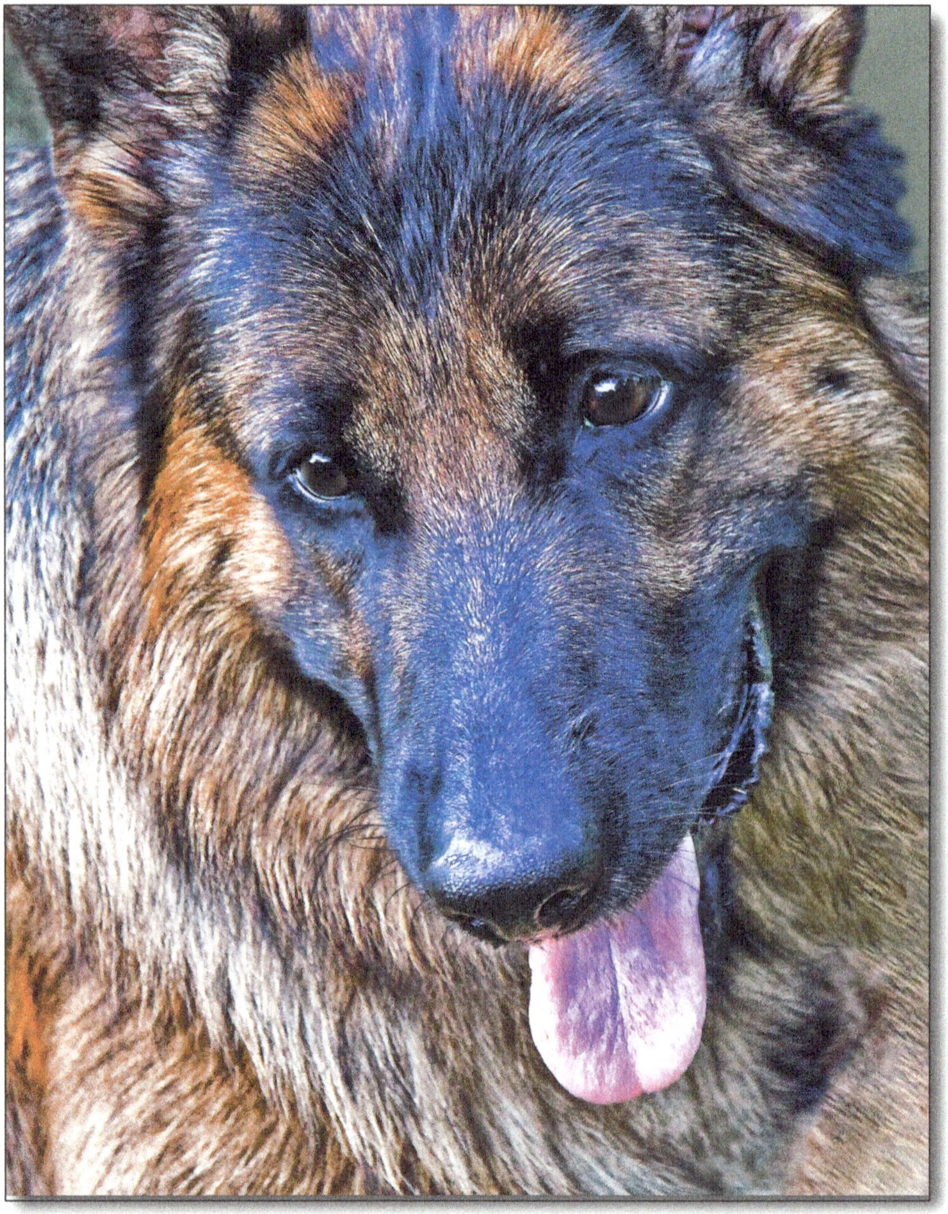

Soldier Service

They were still in the throes of intermittent heartache after the loss of their Shepherd service dog when the doorbell rang. Visibly anxious; her fingers unconsciously wound a stray hair behind her left ear as she turned the doorknob. Two handsome sturdy young males greeted her. Their smiles eased her nervousness. One was a six-foot tall lanky young man and the other stood two feet high on four legs sporting the classic German Shepherd coat. Their new service dog had arrived.

Years ago, Sgt. Patrick Logan was injured by a roadside bomb in Iraq. He still suffers from PTSD (Post Traumatic Stress Disorder) and TBI (Traumatic Brain Injury). When Patrick came home unable to adapt on his own, Mrs. Logan went into action. She found him a dog to assist with his disabilities. Her extensive research enabled her to help train Ranger to accommodate Patrick's needs. Ranger, their first German Shepherd, helped Patrick gain self-confidence mentally, physically and emotionally in just six months. Patrick's dexterity improved by performing activities with his live-in faux Physical Therapy dog. Every Wednesday at 9 a.m. Ranger carried his brush in his mouth to Patrick for the weekly fur brushing ritual.

In a lighthearted mood, Patrick's wife carried her brush in her mouth and crawled on the bed toward him one evening. When she dropped the brush in front of him they broke out in hysterical laughter. Playing games like tug-a-toy and throwing a Frisbee with Ranger expanded Patrick's motor skills. Ranger provided a good listening ear while Patrick practiced reading aloud. His unconditional dedication boosted his master's morale.

Life was good. Ranger was already four years old when the Logans opened their home and heart to him. Shortly after his tenth birthday he passed away, ironically from a brain tumor.

They were devastated. Now somber, they're turning to another German Shepherd named Hefner. Hefner was trained at a canine companion agency. Hopefully he would evolve into the role of Ranger's replacement. The Logans were up for the challenge. They spent days working with Hef. The days turned into weeks. After two months Hefner wasn't catching on to the finer points of Patrick's needs. He was a loving dog, but not as focused as he should be for the animal assistance that was necessary.

They were contemplating their options when a friend of Mrs. Logan's called saying she knew a man whose wife had died suddenly. It was too painful for him to care for her exceptional service dog so he was looking for a home for it. A solution had fallen into their laps! They tried not to get their hopes up. There were a couple of obstacles. This service dog was a female AND a small breed.

Lizzie was an adorable Pomeranian, but she needed to be more than adorable to fill the army booties of Ranger. Would Hefner tolerate Lizzie and visa versa? Would Lizzie bond with Patrick? More importantly would the Sgt. adjust to a 5.5-pound ball of fluff after being supported by a 75-pound muscle dog? Even though they didn't want to waste more time on cultivating a rapport with another canine, they decided to give Lizzie a try. They certainly didn't want her to stay at the other home where she wasn't wanted.

Mrs. Logan picked up Lizzie and all her accessories but was not ready to be mesmerized by her demeanor. Lizzie looked poised and eager for the next mission. She reminded Mrs. Logan of a little soldier. The instant Lizzie paraded into the house, the mood shifted. She commanded everyone's attention. Jumping into Patrick's lap, she gave him the once-over critical eye, evaluating his worthiness of her skills. Everyone held their breath. They saw the furry mouth open to a smile. Lizzie approved. Now it was her turn to pass scrutiny.

Two hours after her arrival and moments before Patrick started to have one of his mild episodes, Lizzie's gentle but decisive paw-tap on his face immediately roused him back to awareness. Small breed dogs do have an advantage. The ability to climb up close and personal allowed Lizzie the insight of imperceptible changes in breathing patterns more efficiently. The Logans were awed.

Lizzie was also a theatrical trick dog. She would balance cookies on her nose and catch them in her mouth while turning a 360. She amused Patrick by catching treats he would randomly throw in her direction.

Mrs. Logan was more amazed by the organizational skills Lizzie could only have learned from her previous charge. It was a sight one had to see to believe. On day two, Lizzie stood on her hind legs and put her front paws on her hips and looked around, appraising the family room. First she marched to the curtains, spiraled the string around one paw and pulled, allowing sunlight to fill the room. The magazines were batted into a perfect fan effect on the coffee table. She scuttled to a cloth wall hanging. When she realized it was beyond her reach she enlisted Hefner to act as her step stool. She jumped on his back and guided him into position, grabbed the edge with her teeth and pulled the tattered décor down with all her might. (The Logans did not spend much time on interior decorating.) Curled up dead flowers were cast to the floor along with their empty vase. Mrs. Logan got the cue and followed Lizzie around picking up the disheveled debris. Lizzie's skills did not stop there. She attacked all the rooms of the house with fervor. Shoes were paired in the bedroom and food bowls rearranged in the kitchen. The Logans were a joyful, orderly unit once again. Even the walls of the house expelled a sigh of relief.

As Lizzie enmeshed herself into the daily routine, Hefner watched and asserted himself where he was best utilized. With Lizzie as the family pack leader, she and Hef provided tandem therapy, service, and entertainment. Sometimes one dog can teach another new tricks. It took two dogs to replace one in their heroic roles to aid a veteran. The soldier service treatment team was a victory.

Oh Poodiful

Oh, Poodiful for spacious skies.

For curly waves of fur

For Poodle mountain majesties

Above the pooted bur

America, America…

TOP TEN PHRASES THAT MAY CONFUSE A DOG

10. I have to cancel guy's night; I am in the doghouse

Dog's reaction: *No way are you sharing my house, you snore too loud, and have man farts.*

9. The cats out of the bag

Dog's reaction: *I don't see any cats, where is the bag?*

8. Don't let the cat outta the bag

Dog's Reaction: *Yes, let the cat out, I will chase it, where is the bag again?*

7. Stand Down

Dog's reaction: *HUH? Do I Stand or do I Down?*

6. That's a load of crap

Dog's reaction: *Don't look at me. I didn't do it.*

5. You're barking up the wrong tree

Dog's reaction: *Is there a right tree to bark up?*

4. It's raining cats and dogs

Dog's reaction: *What are we waiting for? Lets go get wet.*

3. Ya feel me dawg?

Dog's reaction: *So now you think you're Randy Jackson?*

2. It's a dog eat dog world

Dog's reaction: *That's just wrong.*

AND THE NUMBER ONE PHRASE THAT MAY CONFUSE A DOG

1. WHO LET THE DOGS OUT?

Dog's reaction: *I'm not out, I'm in and there are no other dogs here. Who is gonna let me out? I'm ready to go out anytime "Who" is ready to go out!*

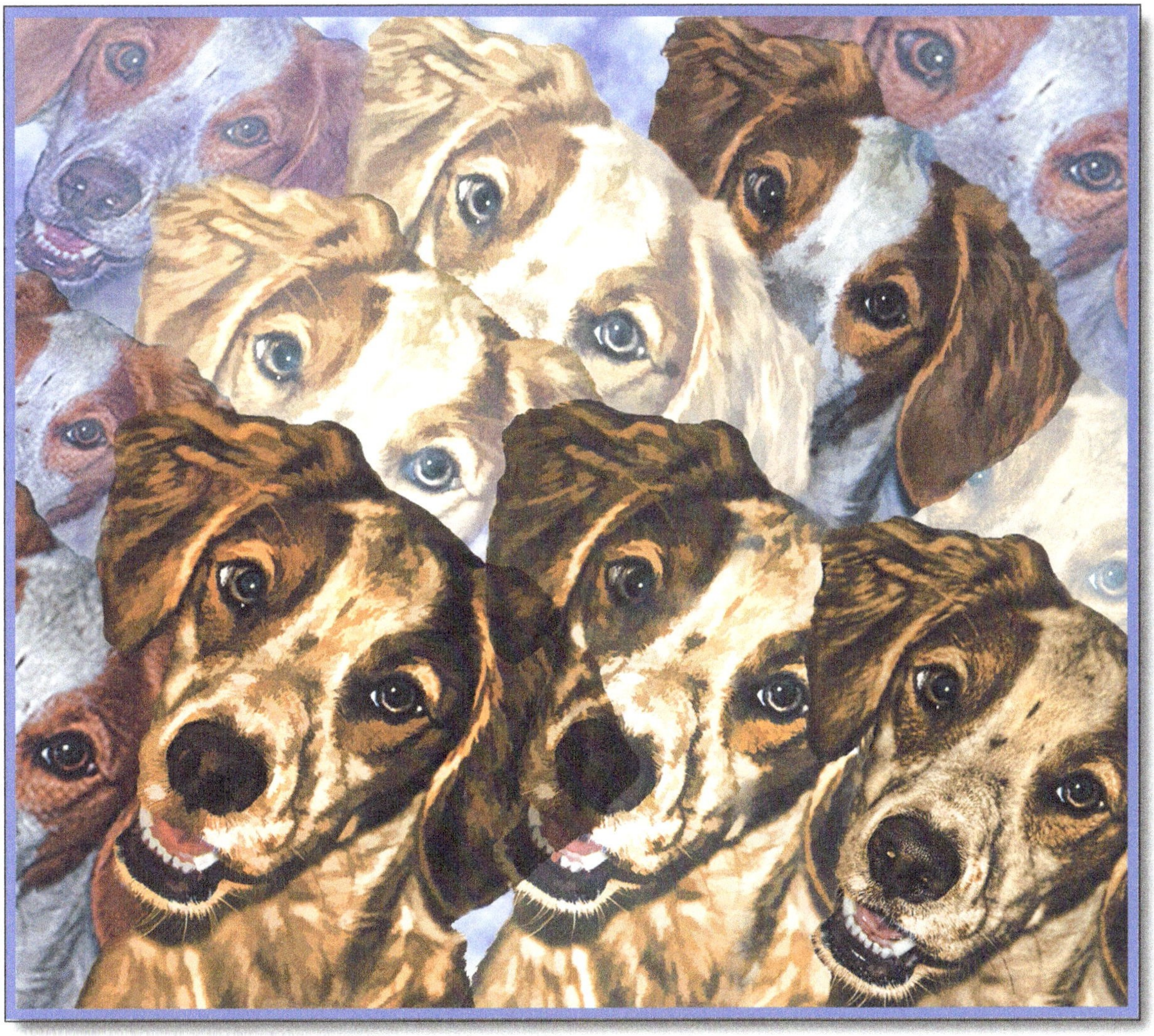

Freedom of Speak

Every morning our country-crooner dog, Loretta, barks to be let out. The other two dogs, Patsy and Willie, join in the chorus with their high-pitch howls. This amusing ritual inside our house never gets old. There was a time when their free spirited canine concerto was forbidden.

We'd moved out of our starter house to a larger one with a fenced yard in an unrestricted neighborhood. After about a year we had everything decorated and landscaped the way we wanted it, UNTIL neighbors moved in behind us…

I arrive home from work and let the dogs out while I change from my work clothes. Loud anxious barking interrupts my routine. I peer out my bedroom window and see the dogs huddled at one end of the chain link fence. Their territory is being threatened. My eyes follow their line of sight. A man is yelling at them from his backyard patio.

I put my work shirt back on and dash outside to pacify the situation. I hush the dogs. Before I can utter an introduction, our new neighbor bellows, "Keep those dang dogs quiet."

"I'm so sorry for the disturbance. They'll settle down after they get used to you being here."

With a grumble, he stalks into his house. *Jeez, that was not an ideal way to make a first impression for either of us.* I jog back into my house to make another attempt to change clothes. From my bedroom, I hear the dogs resume their barking. *Now what?* I look out the window again. The man now lurks on his back porch with a beer screaming at my dogs. In reply to his elevated volume, their barks are louder. *This guy is a real moron, so much for good impressions.* In my comfort clothes, I march with determination to resolve this issue. I round up the trio and secure them inside.

On my way back to the fence, I convince myself to try a proper greeting by offering my name. This six foot two Neanderthal piece a work, growls, "I don't care what the hell your name is Missy, just keep your damn dogs quiet!"

I gather all of my five feet nothing and counter, "You're the one who's provoking them by shouting." He said, "Provoke this," grabbed his male danglers and called me a string of absurd names. Clearly, he is a man with a limited vocabulary. I mutter a feminine hygiene insult and decide right then I would not be offering him any 'welcome to the neighborhood' muffins! Hopefully he has a reasonable wife.

As my husband's truck pulls into the garage, I'm calmer thanks to the effects of a delightful glass (or two) of red wine. I sit him down and fill him in. Incensed, puffs of smoke curl out of his ears, he jumps up, "Fetch my Super X Pump Winchester rifle."

"Rifle? Uh, dear, you don't own a rifle, or any guns for that matter."

He flops back on the couch, "Oh yeah. I hate guns."

We all go together for the after dinner doggie outing. The dogs bark as they race to the back of the fence to exercise their protective curiosity. The new family is outdoors. Our dogs will cease barking once the threat is reduced. But the hellion man and his two kids feed the fury by shrieking at our dogs. The lady of the house retreats inside. *Coward!* Mr. Man throws a large rock at our dogs. *Okay it's a beer koozie. It could have been a rock.*

I mentally load an artillery projectile into our Civil War cannon to retaliate. In reality my husband charges the fence at warp speed. The two men have a macho meltdown of nuclear proportion. At one point El Toro Drunko challenges my husband to settle this dispute the old fashioned way and duke it out. *Darn, I'd just dropped his boxing gloves off at the cleaners. Who knew?* The dogs, not getting any attention, wander off. The men realize they are yelling over soundlessness, and abruptly walk away from each other.

During the next few weeks we avoid the intimidating bullies. The dogs are let out one or two at a time. We assume things are status quo until we find a ticket from animal control tacked to our front door. It's for nuisance barking. My heart races and my hands shake as I drive downtown to their office. I explain the situation (without expletives). They describe the county laws and give me suggestions to avoid further action. I'm hopeful.

Large Palm trees go inside our fence, bushy shrubbery outside and a privacy fence is installed around the chain link. All our efforts to block noise and confrontations make us feel claustrophobic in our own home. Our neighbors reach new heights and appropriate their children's tree house. They sit up there with friends, drinking and laughing as they agitate our animals into a frenzied state.

We outfit the dogs with bark collars as the last defense to keep the peace. As I contemplate building a moat around our fortress, I peruse the mail. I read "NOTICE TO APPEAR IN COURT". *What?* I scream, cry and stomp out a tantrum. They're not going to take our dogs! I gather my soggy tissues and call our attorney for guidance.

I perform my best Stephanie Plum-like investigating techniques and snap 8 x 10 glossy photos. Trampled bushes and crushed flowers between our properties prove that someone has been intentionally provoking our dogs. We audiotape our dogs barking during the day when we aren't home. This establishes they bark less than the allowed length of the time. We enlist the support of our other neighbors and a certified dog obedience and temperament tester. Both are familiar with our dogs and agreed to be in court on our behalf.

The court date arrives, we are armed and dangerous, *more like disarmed and harmless*, but confident. The accusers have an audiotape of dogs barking too. The judge takes the two tapes into his chamber to listen. He declares they are the same dog. *Uh, really?* He slaps us with a frivolous $25.00 fine. I'm ready with my Freedom of Speak speech, but he smacks that gavel and it's over. The tapes are the only admissible evidence. *No speech, no character witnesses, no day in court for us*. We lost. The Losers won and cackle at us as we leave the building. Now what? We continue to live a muffled existence, with the mute button pressed on our lives?

******

It's three months to the day since the sentencing. A beacon of light shines through our dismal tunnel by way of a For Sale sign on the front yard of the dog haters. Our prayers have been answered. The house sells quickly and the new, new neighbors are a blessing.

We visit promptly, welcome muffins in hand. The door opens to a household of earsplitting kids, screeching birds, tanks of flesh eating fish and a flock of smelly chickens. *Oh, my.* We love them.

We can remove the bark collars from our pups. Loretta and her posse are once again allowed the Freedom of Speak!

The Talker

Can we talk? Can we walk where I want to walk? We always walk where you want to walk. Isn't it my walk, a dog's walk? I need to broaden my territory, meet new dogs, pee new bushes, and to see beyond the trees.

O.K. here we go!! Uh this is the same path…good talk, eh, oh well; any walk is better than no walk.

Farm Dog

𝓑asset Hounds are known for their sad eyes and Cyrus was no exception. However, Cyrus had seen enough tragedy to warrant his cheerless look. Cyrus lived on a 75-acre farm in Central Florida. Basset Hounds are not your typical farm dogs, but Cyrus had a gentle, congenial nature and was compatible with the farm animals.

His first taste of heartbreak was with a chicken buddy. It is quite rare for dogs and chickens to co-exist, but Cyrus wouldn't hurt a fly. He and one particularly handsome grass-fed chicken chased each other around the coup daily. One morning the chicken was gone and that night for dinner, Cyrus noticed a serving plate that was covered with poultry that resembled his playmate. It was no surprise that Cyrus didn't eat that night.

Cyrus also spent time with the pigs, since they were his closest dimensional equals. He loved to wallow and roll around in the mud with the piglets. They would grunt and howl out a melody together in not so perfect harmony. He didn't even notice their smell. His owner did and Cyrus wasn't allowed in the house without a thorough washing. Time and time again Cyrus would get attached to a feeder pig and then it would be sold at market.

These losses were small calamities in Cyrus' life compared to losing his most important companions-the boys. During the day, Cyrus was the protector to the youngest son Barton. Cyrus tried to make sure no harm came to Barton by chasing away bees so they didn't sting him or preventing him from a fall in the pond. They spent hours cheering while older brother Baxter performed tricks on his horse. At night after Barton went to sleep, Cyrus transferred his dedicated attention to Baxter and lay by his feet while he watched TV or did his homework.

The day came when it was time for Barton's first day of school. It was a rainy morning and Barton was driven away in the family car. They'll just be gone for a short while, Cyrus thought, so he sat and waited in the rain by the gate. When the car came back with no Barton, Cyrus was confused, bewildered and barked anxiously. He finally calmed down and tried to find answers from the pigs and the chickens. They were clueless. A new layer of sadness weighed heavily on Cyrus' already sorrowful eyes. The next day was the same. At least he had his nights with the boys.

It was foreseeable to everyone but Cyrus that Baxter would be leaving to go away to an Equestrian School to further his skills. When this happened Cyrus sulked and moped around for days, then weeks. Nothing would cheer him up.

On Easter Sunday while Baxter was home visiting, the whole family piled in the car. Cyrus was left to his own devices. The chickens tried to engage him, and the pigs tried to push him in the mud. He was lethargic, unconcerned with time. He lazily lifted his head when he saw the car pull up the driveway. As the family piled out of the car Barton dropped something out of his arms. That something moved, ran up to Cyrus and started sniffing. It was another dog! Cyrus had a playmate. The transformation was magical. Cyrus bared his teeth in a broad smile, wagged his tail and looked at his owners with grateful sad set eyes. Everyone laughed, relieved that Cyrus was his old playful self again. The next day the boys went their respective ways, said their good byes and told Cyrus to have fun with his new girlfriend. They would have bet the farm that Cyrus gave them a wink and trotted off with his new partner in exploration.

Dig It Dog

I wish I had the single-minded focus of my dog when he's on the trail of a scent. Brody is so driven by what he smells that I have researched Scent and Blood Hounds to see if he qualifies. I know he's not purebred but he does seem to have the traits and look of these hounds. He has an incredible level of stamina and Iron Man determination. He'll never give up on finding his prey once he's onto an interesting odor. When his nose starts twitching like Samantha Stevens from Bewitched and he lowers his head to concentrate on the field, that's my cue to tighten up on the leash and hang on for the ride.

My first instinct is to look for a cat or a squirrel but soon Brody starts pawing at the ground and triumphantly uncovers a turtle or a mole. Unlike true Scent Hounds he doesn't bay to alert his owner of his findings, no he wants to stay and play with his bounty. I will never forget the image of a white tail hanging out of Brody's mouth. He was so proud of himself he couldn't wait to share his conquest. When I ordered him to drop it, a dead mouse promptly fell at my feet. What a sweet gift, you shouldn't have, no really you shouldn't have. There was not a scratch on the mouse, poor thing probably died of fright.

One hot sunny day while Brody was in the yard, he started digging next to the fence. He rarely digs. I thought he was once again in pursuit of a ground-dwelling animal. He carved out a half moon shaped bunker, circled around in it a couple of times, plunked down pleased with his handiwork. It kept his belly nice and cool and so did the ice-cold beer he was drinking. (Um, no not really)

The stereotypical dog digs a hole to bury or uncover a possession that has been hidden. It isn't always as simplistic as that. I've had dogs that were escape artists and dug until they were free on the other side. It actually hurt my feelings that they kept digging. Were they trying to get away from me? Were they bored and wanted to see what was on the other side? I tried a variety of different methods to prevent their breakout until I had the boys fixed. They stopped. 'Click' goes the light bulb for me; they were tunneling out to find girlfriends… Duh, slap hand to forehead.

Just like people, some dogs crave the taste of soil or smell of fertilizer. I don't really know any people who delight in dirt al dente but I've heard it could be a sign of mineral deficiency. Here's a tip-don't let your dog go through an airport checkpoint with fertilizer on their paws; they may get detained. It happened to me. I was stopped and frisked at the airport for having a bomb like substance on my shoes, which was really fertilizer.

Certain breeds dig for the pure gratification of digging. They like to get your attention while they tear up the yard and admire their destruction. Then again dog paddling into the earth is a good form of exercise. Did you know that one in three marriages ends in divorce as a result of digging dogs? Actually, I made that up but it could be true. Picture the spouse who had poured many hours, dollars and sweat into the perfectly designed yard. Unbeknownst to them the dogs have dug a crater to the Equator. You notice the gaping hole but decide to keep it a secret. When your spouse asks you if you would like to accompany them for a walk on the beach or a movie, you say, "No Hon, you go on ahead." Your spouse leaves a little apprehensive while you impatiently thrust them out the door. Once they're gone, you rush to fill in the hole with dirt before they notice. Now imagine this happening repeatedly. Their suspicion rises to a feverish, ready-for-a-divorce, pitch! You must confess…and all is forgiven. Well, except for the deep crevices all over the yard.

Whatever a dog's reason is for excavating, they have an unwavering concentration that I would like to harness for myself. Perhaps Brody can dig up a bottle of focus for me.

Saved by the Law

We were laughing while riding our bicycles on the sidewalk when it happened. I put on the brakes fast and hard. I yelled to my friend to get the license plate of the car that slowed down long enough for the degenerate passenger to lob a dog out of the truck window. The road was heavily traveled as a main route through suburban neighborhoods. Two things were plainly obvious; one, the offenders wanted the pooch to be rescued and two; they didn't count on the fact that it would be rescued by a couple of dog loving policewomen.

We were off duty, but that didn't stop us from saving a life and chasing lawbreakers. It appeared that a female had thrown the dog to the side of the road as gently as she could. My heart shattered in pieces when the dog landed and instantly tried to follow the departing vehicle but awkwardly stopped short. When I reached the little pup, she looked so forlorn, whimpering in pain. I stayed with her while my friend dashed to her nearby home, retrieved her car and we took Ali, as her nametag read, to our veterinarian. I cradled her in my arms to immobilize her. My heart splintered again as Ali's fearful eyes searched mine. We rode in silence wondering why anyone would be so malicious.

We left Ali safely sedated overnight for tests and observation. Mercifully, she had only suffered a few cuts and one broken leg. She did have a bruised rib inconsistent with the fall. After another overnighter in the kennel, I took her home with me to continue her emotional and physical healing. What a love, how could anyone discard this cuddle bug?

Now it was time to hunt down the callous, calculating criminals against canines and stick them with a cattle prod. I know what you're thinking, not a severe enough punishment. How about we find the culprits and fry 'em? Two days of tedious scanning of partial plates rewarded us with the location of the vehicle. The pickup was registered to a male who had a restraining order against him from an ex-wife and a battery conviction. There's a shocker.

Florida has laws against intentional cruelty to an animal. The penalty carries a fine up to $10,000 and imprisonment up to five years. We were eyewitnesses, not much allowance for a not guilty plea. My friend and I were anxious to make the collar (no pun intended), but we were taking no chances. Backup was coming with us. A female with a swollen lip answered the door. She gasped when she saw us but allowed us to enter. I glanced around and saw a few dog toys on the floor and a photo of her holding Ali. Through racking sobs she admitted to the felony. Her boyfriend said he would kill the dog if she didn't toss it out the window. Apparently he was jealous because she loved the dog more than him, go figure. She also admitted that he had kicked the dog, thus the bruised rib. As on Judge Judy, justice prevailed, both were convicted and never allowed to own a dog again.

Ali was sentenced to live the rest of her long life with this single mother and her son. At first, she would shy away from all male figures. My son was very gentle and patient with her. She made a full ruff recovery in our caring home. I was never going to abandon our Ali Wali pal.

Beyond Friendly

Don't be ashamed of this look…

Don't be mortified if your sweet little mutt

Runs to another dog and sniffs his butt

It's simply their handshake *Pleased to meet you*

Returning the greeting he looks there too

"Smells like you ate Boeuf Bourguignon for lunch"

"Yeah, that's my favorite out of the whole bunch"

"I'm not sure why I just snorked your behind"

"You'd better move away or that's not all you'll find!"

Dog Trivia

1. What do the following dog breeds have in common?
Maltese   English Setters   Dalmatians   West Highland   Terriers

2. Which one of the following breeds is not considered one of the oldest domestic breeds?
Siberian Husky   Lhasa Apso   Shar Pei   German Sheppard   Pekingese

3. What is the percentage of animal shelter dogs that are euthanized each year? (Best Estimate)
15%   25%   50%   66%   75%

4. How much did Americans spend for Halloween Pet Costumes in 2011?
3 Million   13 Million   31 Million   103 Million   310 Million

5. How many of these foods should you never feed your dog?

Avocado, Beer, Chocolate, Grapes, Macadamia Nuts, Onions
2 of the above   3 of the above   4 of the above   all of the above

Dog Trivia
1. All born white
2. German Shepherd
3. 50% according to the HSUS
4. 310 Million
5. All of the Above

Answers to which dogs were adopted from a shelter/rescue organization.

Check to see how many you got correct! The following were rescued (story name listed first, then the breed, as told to us):

Gloria's Inspiration-Orange Brittany and Liver Brittany Mix

Fern's Inspiration Short Version-Terrier Mix Puppy

Fern's Inspiration Long Version-(from top left) Lab/Terrier Mix, German Shepherd Mix, Bull Terrier, Chocolate Lab, Black Shepherd Mix, Staffordshire Terrier Mix, Hound Mix, Tree Walking Hound, Hound/Lab Mix

Our Child- all Hound Mixes

Salty Dog-Parson Brown Terrier

Joy, Oh Boy-Hound Mix Puppy

Pure Joy-Chihuahua/Lab Mix Puppy

King Size Optimist-Chihuahua Mix Puppy and Lab/Pit Bull Mix

Chubs-Pug and two Bull Dogs

Poo Diddy Poo-Bullmastiff/Boxer Mix **Here's Tony**

Secret's Out-Orange Brittany and English Setter Puppy

Miss Dancer-French Brittany

Charmed, I'm Sure-German Shepherd Puppy

Get a Lil Chi-Chihuahua Puppy Littermates

Captain Snifter Lab Mix

Park It-(dogs in front) Orange Brittany Mix, Cocker Spaniel/Brittany and (dog in rear) Black King Charles Spaniel, (dog sitting on stump) Orange Brittany

The Thinker-Brittany Mix

Fifty Shades of Dachshunds-(elongated full body) tan, (next row up, from left to right) Tri-colored

Dachshunds, (middle) Dachshund/Chihuahua Mix

The Right Match-German Shorthaired Pointer

LBD (not your Little Black Dress)-Rottweiler, both, same dog

In the Habit-German Shepherd Mix

Devoted-Tri-colored Brittany Mix

Blizzard's Adventure-Lhasa Apso Mix

Ole Blue Eyes-Dachshund

Dog Quartet-French Brittany and Hound/Boxer Puppies

Bad Hair Day-Shih Tzu Mix

The Aww Factor-Hound Terrier

Canine Couriers-Tree Walking Hound and Pointer

Aww Factor Number 2-Hound Puppy Mix

Dog Art-Brittany

Beach Discovery- Bullmastiff/Boxer Mix**Here's Tony**

Service Soldier-Pomeranian

Top Ten Phrases-French Brittany

Freedom of Speak-Liver Springer/Brittany and Rat Terrier Mix

The Talker-Miniature Pincher

Farm Dog-Lab Mix

Dig It Dog-Beagle

Saved by the Law- Shih Tzu/Lhasa Apso Mix

Lovitude-Cocker Spaniel

End of Series-Jack Russell/Terrier Mix

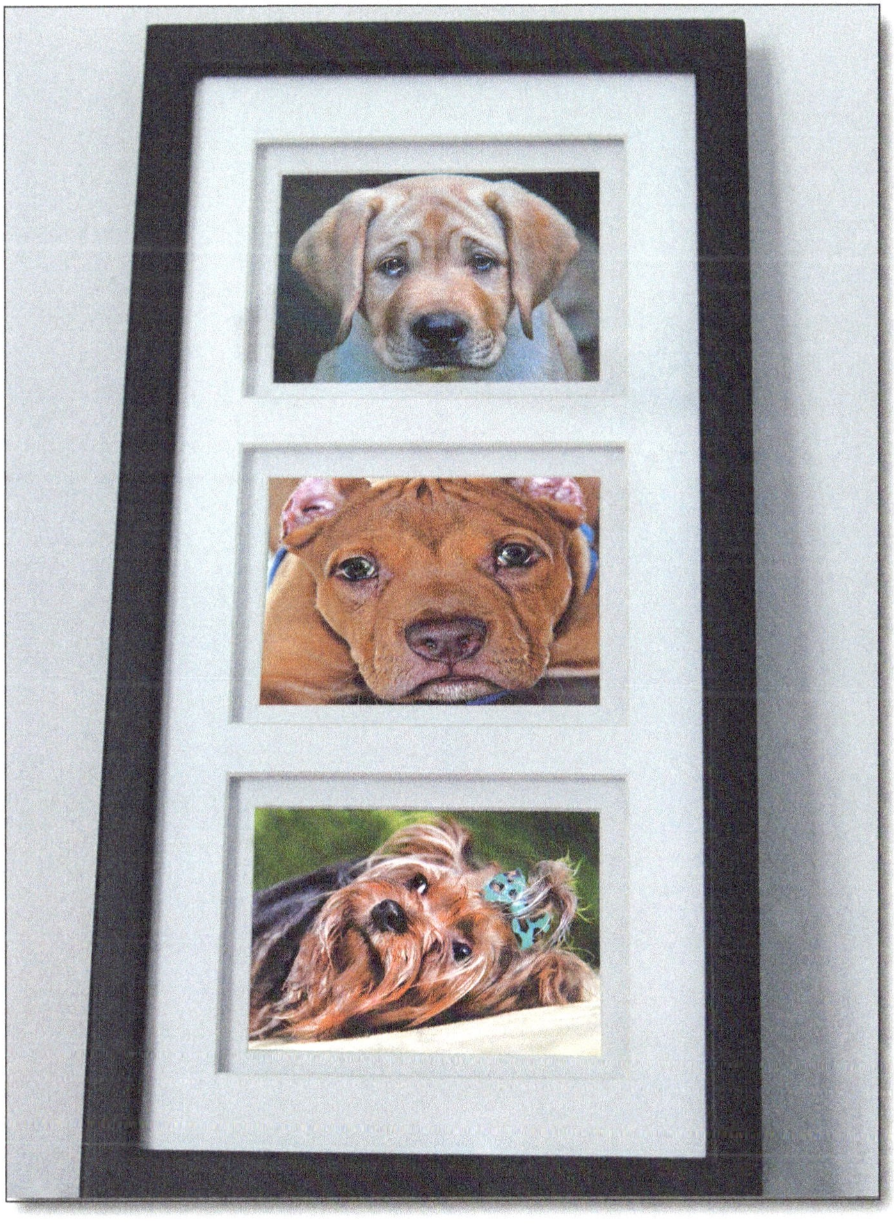

Lovitude

*I*t's all about the look that transpires between a loyal dog and his master. The look from your dog that melts the butter, curls the toes, sweetens the coffee, and makes you scrunch your face into an awww…he/she loves me so very much. The look of Love mixed with Gratitude. A mesmerizing gaze called lovitude.

This happens when…

…you bring home a new squeaky toy; he grabs it, whips it around then takes a moment to look up at you with lovitude.

…getting ready to leave in the morning, snatch up your keys, your cell phone, your travel mug, gather up your files. Don't forget to crate the dog! Run to the bedroom, calling her name, run to the kitchen, not there either. There she is waiting in her kennel looking to you grateful for her safe home. That's lovitude.

…you come home late; you know Sparkle is busting to go out. The first thing you do is open the door to the backyard, she should be mad but she looks up at you with what? Lovitude.

…you see him digging a hole; you shake your head "no." He looks at you, knows he was bad; he comes running to you and gives you what look? The look of lovitude, cuz you didn't yell at him, how could you when he looks at you that way?

…it's been a few days, you ask your dog if he wants to go for a car ride, he looks at you, "does a bear shit in the woods?" That's lovitude.

…when you locate your dogs' special scratch spot they lean into you for continuous bliss. They communicate lovitude.

…letting your dog sleep wherever on whatever-that's lovitude too.

Send us your experiences of lovitude to thelookofthedog@hotmail.com

check out websites

ferngoodman.com and gloriayarina.com

End of Series

You have reached the end of this series

We want to hear your dog ideas or queries

Write down your stories or type them up

Snail mail or email us about your pup

Just send us the text no photographs please

If we use your submission, you'll sign a release

We plan to keep writing many more of these books

Because dogs keep delighting us with all their looks

The Dogs: Big Tony, Sonny and Lady

The Chicks: Fern and Gloria

Not Pictured; Jen

The love of dogs rekindled the estranged relationship between Fern and Gloria. These two gals, sisters by birth, grew up in Michigan years apart. Now in Florida with 118.6 miles separating them, they collaborated on this book together.

Fern's stories have been published in a Florida Writers Book of Collections, magazines and newsletters. Gloria's pet photographs hang on many home walls, adoption agency literature and are highlighted in *Food for Thought: Recipes for Brittany's and their People.*

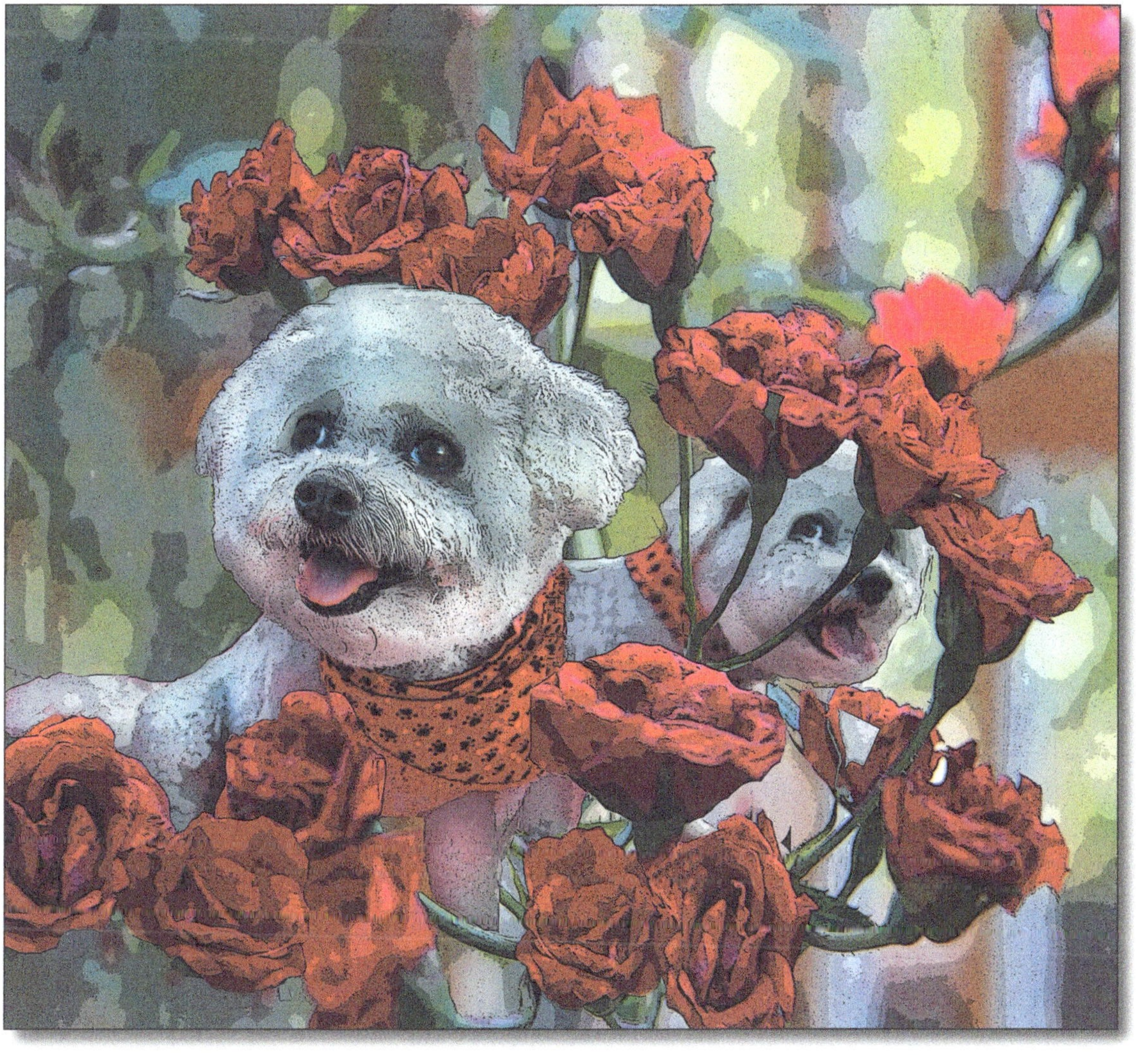

CPSIA information can be obtained at www.ICGtesting.com
Printed in the USA
LVOW02s0250121114

413262LV00003B/11/P

9 781457 532078